Reinvent Your Impact: Unleashing Purpose, Passion and Productivity to Thrive!

Chuck Bolton

Bestselling Author

The Reinvention Solution Publishing

Reinvention
the Solution

A Note of Gratitude

This book is dedicated to my Fabulous Fourteen who inspire me to live a life of impact.

That's Mary, John, Jordan, Jack, Sarah, Danny, Theo, Alli, Derek, Mollie, Lucie, Nick and Jack, who along with me, make up our Fabulous Fourteen. I love you all and pray you'll always live lives of impact.

Without Mom and Coach John LaSage, this book wouldn't have been possible. Thank you for showing me the way when it mattered most.

I also owe a debt of gratitude to Renee Skiles for her editing and Justin Morison for his illustrations. No one walks alone.

Most of all, a big thank you to you, as you commit to living a life of impact. When you live a life of impact – and it's never too early or too late to live a life of impact – we all benefit. Make the commitment!

Table of Contents

Chapter 1: Create Great Impact

"I've Got a Problem…"

When I woke up that Wednesday morning in late October and saw the text message sent at 2:13 am by Jack Morgan, one of my clients, I knew something important was up.

His message read, "Hi Chuck: I've got a problem and could use your help. Can you call me in the morning? Thanks. Jack"

That wasn't the way Jack typically communicated. When he needed something, he called me directly. And at that early hour - something was weighing heavily on him.

I wondered what was up. Work? Personal? Something else?

A little background. Three years ago, Jack was hired as the president of large division for a global medical technology company. Jack initially asked me to work with his team as they created a strategic blueprint to grow the business. A year after that, to get everyone across the organization focused, aligned and producing massively on the company's most important goals, they launched an Objectives and Key Results (OKR) system, and I helped him on the implementation. Since then, I provided individual coaching for several of his executives.

Jack had a big job – an important role – and the compensation to match. From all indications, he was well thought of at work.

Every time we spoke, Jack raved about his wife, Kiki, and their two kids. He obviously adored his family. So, from the outside in, Jack had a good, happy life. Yet, we all know that looks can be deceiving sometimes.

At 7:00 am, I sent Jack a text with my availability that morning. Five seconds after hitting the send button, my phone buzzed. It was Jack.

He asked, "Do you have a few minutes?"

I answered affirmatively, and he got right to the point, skipping the social niceties.

"Where do I start? Here's the bottom line. I've hit the wall. I think it may be time for me to move on."

A moment of silence.

"That's big, Jack. Keep talking." I said.

"How long has it been since we last spoke? Six months or so?" Jack asked.

"That sounds about right," I replied.

"OK, since we last talked, my team has been putting up the numbers. We're having a solid year, and we'll make our sales and profit plan numbers when the year wraps up in a few months, barring any unforeseen crisis."

Jack continued, "Here's the thing. I think the problem is me. I've been running divisions for big companies nearly fifteen years, and it's becoming a grind. It's not just one thing – it's a lot of things."

"This whole annual cycle is wearing me down. Create the strategic plan, develop an annual operating budget. Nonstop monthly meetings and reviews. Set the pace. Get people aligned to execute. Push, push, push. Performance reviews and succession planning. Quarterly offsite meetings for corporate. Offsite meetings with my team every quarter, too. Travel around the world twice a year. One conference after another. Too many overnights away from home. Finish the year. Repeat. It's getting old. I don't think others see me grinding at work. I hope they aren't seeing it. But I'm struggling and I don't see a clear way out of it."

Jack continued, "I don't know quite how to describe it, but something is missing. It's frustrating. I feel adrift. Like I'm going through the motions. Spinning my wheels. I don't like it. I'm not getting juice from my work."

"I've been feeling this way for over six months. It's a gnawing feeling that isn't getting better. I feel like I'm surviving but not thriving. I just don't know how to get out of this rut – this funk."

He continued, "I'm bringing it home, too. Is this a mid-life crisis, I've wondered? I wouldn't call it a mid-life crisis. I love Kiki to pieces and my family, but it feels like a career crisis. Like I've hit the wall. Kiki is getting tired of hearing me complain. By the way, she was the one who mentioned you might have some ideas. She suggested I call you."

Jack continued, "Maybe it's because I just turned fifty-three. My dad died at fifty-five. That was thirty years ago. Dad was a manager at Bethlehem Steel. He got laid off at fifty, never found another job, and died of a heart attack, frustrated and cynical. I'm knocking on the door of the age Dad was when he passed. I'd like to work another ten years if I can. Yet I know life is short and time is ticking."

He commented, "I feel a little guilty complaining. From a material standpoint, I am fortunate. Many people would like to trade places and have my job and life. I'm grateful for what I have, but I'm not getting the juice I want or need from work. It's left me wrestling with a lot of questions."

"And what are those questions?" I asked.

"Well, here are some that are on my mind," and he listed off four:

- How do I break out of this funk?
- Do I still have what it takes?
- Is this what I am meant to be doing?
- Am I living my truth?

Jack admitted, "I don't know the answers, but I'm feeling a void. Something's missing."

I responded, "These are big, existential questions. These are questions that just about everyone grapples with at some point in their lives. How do you get those answered?"

Jack hesitated, "Here's what I'm thinking. The way I see it, I have three options. First, maybe it's time for something new. One option is to resign, take some time off and figure out what I really want to do for the rest of my life. What do you think?"

I replied to him, "That certainly is an option. Would you see that as running from what you've been feeling, though? What are the other options you're considering?"

"Second, I don't have to resign. I can start looking for another job. Start my job search quietly. I get a fair number of calls from recruiters and have a decent network I can tap into. I haven't been looking for a new job, but I believe I could find one if I put my mind to it. Maybe a new challenge would get me fired up again."

I said, "That's also an option. What's the other option?"

"I can grin and bear it. Keep grinding this thing out and hope things get better in time."

I replied, "That's yet another option. Anything else?"

Jack paused for thirty seconds or so.

"Or, maybe I reach out to someone who has some other ideas and we talk a bit. Maybe help me see things differently."

Jack concluded, "Those are my choices as I see them. What do you think?"

Reflecting for a moment, I replied, "Jack, you can try to escape from the tension of your work, you can take off and go to an island and contemplate life, you can quit your job and go somewhere else, or you can grind things out and hope things will improve.

"But until you get some answers for yourself to those questions you are wrestling with, you'll find that your problem is one that you will continue to take with you. It's going to follow you.

The good news is you own both this problem and the answers, too. From my experience, you don't have to decide to quit your job and the company — at least not now — to get the answers to those questions. The tension you are feeling is a call that you need to take action."

Silence on the other end of the phone. Then I heard a big sigh.

"Let me ask you a question, Jack. If you had to put your finger on it, in one or two words, what are you really seeking?"

He thought for a second and then replied, "Meaning. And impact. Yes. Meaning and impact. I want to feel more meaning, like my work and life is making a real difference. Does what I'm doing really mean anything? I'd like to know that I'm having impact."

I responded to Jack, "Then it sounds like you are experiencing a meaning and impact void. Is that a fair assessment?"

"That is fair! That's how I'm feeling." he replied.

"If you could get clear on how to get more meaning from work and how to create greater impact, would that be a win? To get more meaning and purpose from work? To get that juice – your passion – back? To feel and be more productive, so you could spend more time on the things in life most important to you? Is that what you're looking for?"

"Yes, yes, yes, and yes!" Jack responded.

"It sounds like you are telling yourself a story about your career and maybe life right now that doesn't fit you well.

"Agreed!" he said.

I asked him, "Do you think you should change that story?"

He paused for a second to let it soak in. He asked, "Yes. Can you help me with that? How soon can we get started?"

We talked through a few details and ended our call.

And then the work began with Jack.

And now our work begins. In this book, I'll be your guide. Your coach. Together, let's reinvent your impact.

What I'm going to share with you is a process you can use to transform your work and life. Up until now, this process – I call it the *Reinvent Your Impact* process – was only available to my individual coaching clients whose companies sponsor our work together. They pay a steep fee so that their executives become the best versions of themselves and create great impact. You are about to discover the same process, simply for the price of this book.

Throughout this book, I'll share with you stories, not only of Jack Morgan, but of many other people who've created and are creating great impact. Some of these people you've heard of, but most are regular folks, like you and me. You may never have heard of them, but they are living lives of impact that make the world a better place.

As we get underway, I'll talk with you as though we are working together one-on-one – just as I do with my individual coaching clients. I see myself coaching you and I promise to give you my best as your coach.

Your end of the deal is you need to do your best, too. Your part is to do the work. There are many questions I'll be asking you along the way, so it's a must that you do the work. You'll create a story and plan to create greater impact. Then, it's your job to put that plan into place so your impact story becomes your reality.

You'll need to write in a journal – what I call a logbook – any time I ask you a question for reflection or assign you a task. If you don't, you simply won't get the results. And neither of us will be happy.

Not unlike a ship captain who uses a logbook to track their journey, you need a logbook to track yours. To write, draw, and enter the story of your reinvention.

A good, inexpensive logbook is the 8.5" x 11" hardbound sketchbook that can be found on the Blick website. I go through several of these each year on my own journey.

Why a logbook, you may ask? What's wrong with a tablet, smart phone or a laptop? Here's why.

Writing in longhand is important for creativity and retention. Holding and moving the pen sends feedback signals to the brain, creating "motor memory." It stimulates synapses between the left and right hemispheres (which does not happen in typing) that make you more creative and thoughtful. So, sit in your comfortable chair, turn on some relaxing music if you like and get busy.

Don't just be interested in what you are reading. *Be committed.* Do the work as though you paid big bucks for me to coach you – just like my CEO clients for an entire year. If you did that, would you be committed? Of course, you would. So, that's the way you must operate throughout our time together as we go step-by-step to reinvent your impact.

When you do this, and you declare and make a commitment, you'll become the hero of your story.

You'll reinvent your impact.

P.S. If you can't wait to discover how Jack Morgan navigated through these choppy waters, you can find his story – *Doing Well by Doing Good* – in Appendix 4.

Impact Defined

Impact is defined as having a strong, powerful effect or influence on a situation or a person.

And make no mistake about it. You are here to have a great impact in this world. You were born to make an impact.

Your purpose is to make a positive difference in the world. When you are making an impact, you flourish.

You are on this earth to flourish – to thrive. When you thrive, others benefit, as they are encouraged and positively impacted by you.

Sociologists tell us the most introverted of people will influence 10,000 in an average lifetime. Imagine how many people you will have knowingly and unknowingly influenced in your life so far.[1]

Are you claiming your purpose and having an impact? Or are you not?

When you don't, you languish. Languishing is the absence of mental and emotional vitality.

Where are you today?

Creating impact is a strategy for playing offense with your life.

If you aren't feeling positively about your work – where you spend 50% or more of your waking hours – it's hard to feel like you are making an impact in the world.

Isn't that what you want? Isn't that what life is all about, to make a positive difference in the world? To make an impact?

Creating impact at work is not just for the rich, wealthy, and powerful. Impact is not about position or title. And it's not about age.

You can make a greater impact in any job, at any level of your organization, and at any age. This is about making a conscious decision about creating impact by becoming a person of consequence. This is about reintroducing you to yourself. You have a lot of pent-up potential to make a bigger impact. It's just dying to get out! In many ways, you're not unlike Jack Morgan.

But there is a villain that seeks to prevent you from making an impact. You've got to know this mighty adversary so you can prevent it from derailing you. You have to be able to identify it and kick its ass.

The Enemy of Impact

There's a villain to defeat. A clear and present danger. And it's got a name. While its name doesn't sound dangerous, it is. It can literally hijack your life. This threat, this villain, is comfort.

Most people have two lives. The first life is the one you are likely living. That's the life of comfort. Then there is the life that is likely unlived within you. That's the life of impact.

Comfort is alluring. She'll seduce you and make you default to her. If you've not made the commitment to impact, comfort has you in her sights, with her fangs out, ready to strike when you falter. Comfort may already have you in her grip.

When you default to comfort, here's what happens. You become bored, disengaged, distracted, and adrift. You play small ball. You live a life that's reactive, shallow, and busy. You may even appear successful on the surface. But you are not the person you could be, and deep down, you know it.

You live a shadow life. You know you are capable of more. You find yourself frustrated, accomplishing little, repeating the daily grind. The same old, same old. You're surviving but not thriving. You may have the means, but you have no meaning.

Does this sound familiar?

A person who defaults to comfort goes through the motions. Bored and disconnected, you become addicted to comfort. Then you become incapacitated by other addictions to get an instant gratification. These addictions can come in many forms. Shopping, excessive social media, punching the clock, procrastination, too much TV and screen time, alcohol, drugs, food, sex, to name several.

The life of comfort becomes the life of an addict. You surrender your power and sabotage yourself. It's an unhappy life.

Comfort disguised like this is actually a false sense of comfort. You may be just one event from losing what you perceive as comfort. Do you think you are comfortable in your high-paying job with a lot of perks? A job loss, a broken relationship, or illness could mightily alter this so-called comfort. Those who opt for comfort are the repeaters. They do what they've always done. Rarely learning or growing and never reinventing. They operate like amateurs. And time is ticking. Never be OK with comfort.

There's a theme song for those who choose comfort. It's appropriately titled, *Comfortably Numb*, performed by the iconic rock band, Pink Floyd. Here are the lyrics:

Hello? Hello? Hello?
Is there anybody in there?
Just nod if you can hear me
Is there anyone at home?
Come on now
I hear you're feeling down
Well I can ease your pain
Get you on your feet again
Relax
I'll need some information first
Just the basic facts
Can you show me where it hurts?
There is no pain you are receding
A distant ship, smoke on the horizon
You are only coming through in waves
Your lips move but I can't hear what you're saying
When I was a child I had a fever
My hands felt just like two balloons
Now I've got that feeling once again
I can't explain you would not understand
This is not how I am

I have become comfortably numb
Okay
Just a little pinprick
There'll be no more, ah
But you may feel a little sick
Can you stand up?
I do believe it's working, good
That'll keep you going through the show
Come on it's time to go
There is no pain you are receding
A distant ship, smoke on the horizon
You are only coming through in waves
Your lips move but I can't hear what you're saying
When I was a child
I caught a fleeting glimpse
Out of the corner of my eye
I turned to look but it was gone
I cannot put my finger on it now
The child is grown
The dream is gone
I have become comfortably numb

What do you do if you find yourself in comfort's grasp? <u>You have to make a choice.</u> Choose to live a life of impact – from this day forward.

What about you? Are you comfortably numb?
Are you addicted to comfort?

When you choose to live a life of impact, you put yourself on a path to flourish. You make an intentional choice to live differently. You choose clarity and focus. You discover yourself. You live a life that is proactive, deep, and meaningful. You mine for and discover your purpose. You are passionate and committed about making a difference. You craft your role. You are productive and you create value for others. You commit to creating impact, growing as a person, and reinventing yourself. You operate like a professional.

"They are the ones who take designing their lives in their own fists—to pursue their heart's calling and make it work." Stephen Pressfield, *The War of Art*

It's an uncertain life, this life of impact. No one – including you – knows where it will take you or the impact you'll create.

Here's what I do know. If you default to comfort, you won't make an impact.

Then, days, months, and years from now, you will regret that you didn't choose impact. That realization will be devastating.

What is the price you'll pay if you choose comfort?

What opportunities will you miss because you've failed to choose impact?

As Jim Rohn so aptly states,

"Potential underutilized leads to pain."

You've got the potential. Let's utilize it.

The Impact Void

Remember the definition of impact. Impact is defined as having a strong, powerful effect or influence on a situation or a person.

Now it's time to get on the proverbial impact scale. Score yourself. On a scale of 1 to 10, with one being low and ten being high, how much of an impact are you creating today?
Your score: _____
If you're like most people, you likely didn't score a 9 or a 10. You know there's more impact to be made. Maybe you are fighting the good fight against comfort, or maybe you've just surrendered.

Again, you can decide today to make a different decision. It's never too late. Plenty of people who are profiled in this book have made or are making a big impact later in life.

People and situations are being impacted powerfully every day, all around the world. How much of an impact are you having? Reflect for a moment. Could you have more impact? My guess is the answer is yes.

It's sad and a waste of potential and talent when an individual trades impact for comfort.

Multiply this by millions and it breaks my heart. Consider the following:

A New York Times article entitled, *"Americans Are Among the Most Stressed People in the World, Poll Finds,"* reported that that in 2018, Americans felt stress, anger, and worry at the highest levels in a decade. The assertion is based on an annual Gallup poll. Specifically, 55% of American adults said they had experienced stress much of the day, just the day before. This is compared with only 35% globally.[3]

These findings are disturbing, disappointing, and another piece of discouraging news about the well-being of Americans. These folks are suffering from negative stress and an absence of vitality. They are clearly not making an impact.

Consider the engagement levels of workers that Gallup reports on every year. Their most recent study showed a whopping 67% of people are either unengaged or disengaged at work. That's two-thirds of the American people! And this has been – more or less – the pattern for the last two decades. It is such a waste of potential and opportunity. It is a huge personal cost for individuals and a huge monetary cost for companies. They aren't having an impact.[4]

We know many don't feel like they are making an impact. Consider all the studies that show a decline in well-being.

- Only 12.3% are passionate about their work.[5]
- 53% of people unhappy at work.[6]
- 61% feel the pace of technological change is moving too fast and they are no longer in control of their destiny.[7]
- 83% of employees worry about losing their jobs.[8]

It's fair to say we have an impact crisis in our country. Millions and millions are not having the impact they are capable of. They aren't claiming their gifts, purposes or passions in productive pursuit of something bigger than they are.

Individually, they experience an impact void. Collectively, we experience impact voids in families, schools, workplaces, churches, cities, states, and countries around the world.

But it doesn't have to be this way.

What happens when you fail to create the impact you're capable of creating? Suffering. Here are three ways suffering occurs when you don't create the impact you have the potential to create.

<u>1. Your well-being suffers</u>
People who create great impact aren't perpetually stressed. They aren't disengaged at work or in life. And they aren't unhappy. They live and work on purpose. The biggest difference between those who create impact and those who don't is that those who create it

have "righted" their lives. They've seized control of their time, energy and focus. They have taken control of their agenda.

2. Your family, friends, and co-workers suffer

When you choose the path of comfort, or if you are apathetic about creating impact, your family, friends, and co-workers suffer. They look to you. They look to you to lead them. And what do they see? What have you taught them through your example? Whichever path you choose, you are teaching them. Will those lessons contribute to them leading a thriving and flourishing life?

It's especially important that you encourage your children to lead a life of impact. The best way you can do this is to be a good role model of someone who feels and lives with a sense of purpose. Appendix 3 – *Encourage Purpose in Your Children* – is a must read for anyone who has kids or is helping shape the lives of children.

3. The world suffers

While living a life of comfort, your unique gifts, your purpose, and your passion—all the good stuff deep within you—will never see the light of day. Whether you appreciate it or not, you are one of a kind. The world misses your contribution and it suffers – in ways small and possibly large – because you didn't choose impact.

"Why, having been endowed with the courageous heart of a lion, do we live as mice?"
Brendon Burchard, The Motivation Manifesto

What is your current story? Are you having the impact that you must? What will your story be in one year? How about in ten years?

A new decade has just begun. Think back to where you were and what you were doing in 2010. For most of us, it seems like yesterday. That's what 2020 will look like in 2030. Before you know it, 2030 will be here. Those ten years are coming, one way or another, whether you like it or not. So what if you embraced this decade? To make a declaration, to make a plan, to make this decade the one where you create greater impact than ever before? To operate at your best?

17

*"Aim to be great in 10 years.
Build health habits today that lead to a great body in 10 years.
Build social habits today that lead to great relationships in 10 years.
Build learning habits today that lead to great knowledge in 10 years.
Long-term thinking is a secret weapon."* James Clear, *Atomic Habits*[9]

I have two requests of you. My first request is to ask you to read this book, do the work I invite you to do, and live a life of great impact. You can do this. I'll show you how.

Secondly, I request you show and encourage others how to create lives of impact. This is when you know you are creating impact: when you help improve the lives of others and they create more impact.

Do these two things and you will live a life of impact, my friend. You will be a person of consequence.

What your decision will be means everything.

Be brave. Choose impact!

"You can choose courage, or you can choose comfort, but you cannot choose both,"
Brene Brown

The Impact Formula

There's a formula for creating impact. When you apply this formula with rigor, just watch what happens!

The formula consists of three elements: Purpose, Passion, and Productivity. None of the elements by themselves will get you the impact you're capable of making. But when combined together, you can see a multiplicative, exponential effect.

Here it is:

Purpose x Passion x Productivity = IMPACT

Here's what you'll get out of this book. Your first step is to get clear about what you see as a successful life. Then you'll determine the unique gift you bring to the world. Everybody has a unique gift, but many don't know what it is or how to apply it. I'll help you pinpoint that unique gift.

Then you'll grab your proverbial pick and shovel and mine for your purpose. You will discover it. You will write your purpose statement and story. I'll demonstrate how you can add jet fuel to your purpose by making a commitment and tapping into your passions and propelling it forward.

If you work for a living, I'll give you a process to recraft your role so that you can create greater value by bringing more purpose, passion, and your uniqueness to your work. Then I'll show you world-class, proven techniques to dramatically improve, and turbocharge your personal productivity.

Finally, to pull it all together, I'll take you through the steps to create your personal impact story. Just like I do for my C-suite level executive coaching clients. Because we're committed to long-term impact, not just a short burst of impact, I'll invite you to prepare a 10-year impact declaration, so you can keep yourself on-course and impact-focused.

Put in your work, stay committed and live a life of greater impact. That's why you're here, right?

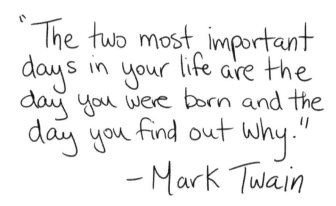

"The two most important days in your life are the day you were born and the day you find out why."
— Mark Twain

No matter where you are in life, no matter your age, you can live and operate purposefully, passionately, and productively to have a great impact.

But here's the caveat. No book is a silver bullet for creating impact. You have to do the work. If you don't, you won't thrive. If you put in the work, you'll be on the road to thrive and to flourish. What do you say we get started?

"I'm Just a Prisoner of Rock and Roll!"

He was born into an unstable environment.

The product of an anxious and chaotic life.

Despite the best efforts of his loving and supportive mother, he lived in a turbulent home. He and his two siblings were raised in a working-class Catholic family in New Jersey. Their uncommunicative father was a bus driver and suffered from mental illness while their mother worked as a legal secretary. As the five of them bounced from one run-down house to another, his mother struggled mightily—through sheer willpower—to keep her small family together.

At the age of seven, he received an inexpensive guitar for Christmas. He taught himself to play songs, even falling asleep at night with it cradled in his arms. He then began writing songs and playing them for his family. After seeing Elvis on *The Ed Sullivan Show,* he knew what he wanted to do with his life. He committed himself to rock and roll as the path out of chaos. He had dreams and visions, fueled by a trait he shared with his mother: willpower.

He dreamed of escaping his roots and small town. In his teens and early 20s, he played in several bands before finally starting his own. And with great effort, persistence, and a bit of good fortune, he got his first small record deal.

He continued working hard, traveling up and down the eastern seaboard, playing bars and small venues. Despite all the hard work, his albums didn't sell. Two years later in 1974, with his recording career in serious jeopardy, he and his band got a lucky break. A photographer known to a local concert promoter suggested booking him for a show. The promoter acted on the recommendation and booked him and his band to open Bonnie Raitt's upcoming concert at Harvard Square Theatre in Cambridge, Massachusetts. Previously, there had been no opening act scheduled the evening of Raitt's concert.

In the audience that evening was a music critic for *Rolling Stone* magazine, Jon Landau.[10] What Landau witnessed that night, and would write about on May 9, 1974, would change the young rocker's life forever. One sentence in his review set the music world on fire and would be repeated in the press for years to come:

> *"I saw the future of rock and roll and its name is Bruce Springsteen."*
> John Landau

One year later, "Born to Run" was released. In addition to the title track, the album featured songs such as "Thunder Road," "Tenth Avenue Freeze-Out," and "Jungleland." Shortly after the collection hit record stores, Springsteen appeared on the covers of *Time* and *Newsweek* magazines – in the same week! Bruce Springsteen and the E-Street Band took off like a rocket!

Bruce Springsteen became one of the biggest names and iconic figures in rock and roll in the last forty-five years, making an enormous impact on music, culture, and the lives of millions of fans. Known as one of the hardest working people in the business, his concerts typically last four hours – whether he's playing a stadium with 60,000 people or in any one of his 236 sold-out performances in 2017 and 2018, *Springsteen on Broadway*, at the Walter Kerr Theatre in New York City.

Have you ever seen Bruce Springsteen in concert? "The Boss," as he is known by his fans, always gives 100% during every performance. You may want to check out *Springsteen on Broadway,* which is now available on Netflix, and see for yourself. There is one point in each performance when the band dramatically stops playing and Bruce screams into the microphone, "I'm just a prisoner of rock and roll!"[11]

From the day he committed to becoming a musician, he has been obsessed and relentless about sharing his music with the world. He's refused to let anything stand in his way. He's pursued his purpose with unbridled enthusiasm. Ultimately, he became one of the top rock artists of our time.

At age 70, Springsteen still performs to sold-out crowds. What drives Springsteen to continue to tour? He answers, "What else would I do? I do it because of the way it makes me feel. It gives me meaning, it gives me purpose," Springsteen explains. "It's the music I can't live without."[12]

Bruce Springsteen is a prisoner of rock and roll. That's his purpose. You know the impact he has had in his career.

What are you the prisoner of?

Do you commit yourself to your work like Bruce Springsteen does to his? What if you did? What if you committed yourself to your craft like Bruce Springsteen does to his?

Watching Springsteen perform makes me want to recommit myself maniacally to my work. To be on fire and work and live on purpose. To operate with great passion. It makes me want to be so productive, passionate and purposeful, so I can make a huge impact and lead a flourishing life.

Don't you want that for your life? Doesn't everyone who wants to flourish want that?

Perhaps you are thinking: "I'm not special. I'm not Bruce Springsteen! I'm just a regular person!"

If that is your belief, or if you are believing or self-talking something similar, you are selling yourself short.

You are special. You are unique. You do have a purpose. It's never too early or too late. You don't need to be a celebrity. You don't need to cure cancer or make a great discovery or create the next killer app or do something that casts you in the public spotlight. You can have a purpose and great impact as a "regular person." In doing so, you'll become someone who has an impact on something or someone. You just have to commit.

If you aren't the prisoner of something, if you don't have something to fight for to give your life meaning, if you don't have a defined purpose, then you can't make the great impact on the world you've been born to make. If you don't have purpose, then you can't make a mark that is uniquely yours.

One of the myths is the "I'm too young" lie. Consider the story of Ryan Hreljac, who at age six, learned in school that many people in

Africa didn't have clean water. In one year, Ryan raised $2,000 to build a well in Uganda. Two years later and he had raised $61,000 for building wells and his story went viral. His parents helped him create a foundation and years later, his foundation brought clean water to nearly one million people with over twelve hundred water and sanitation projects. You can read more about his story and how to assist your children in finding a purpose and creating an impact in Appendix 3.[13]

Or, maybe you think time has passed you by—the "I'm too old" lie. You've felt like you've "Missed my opportunity" or "It's too late" to make an impact. Forget about it! The examples of older people who have found their purpose and are making an impact are endless. Here are a few examples.

Julia Child released her first cookbook at 39 and didn't get her first cooking show until age 51. Samuel L. Jackson didn't get his first movie role until he was 46. Morgan Freeman didn't get his first major movie role until age 52. Louise Bourgeois didn't become a famous artist until she was 78. So never tell yourself you are too old to make an impact. Or that you missed your chance. Or that you aren't good enough.

You can make an impact. I'll show you how. <u>First, you make the decision to make an impact.</u> Just like Jim Conn has made an impact in his encore career.

<u>"For the First Time in His Life, He Was Able to Get Around..."</u>

The old factories and warehouses that powered the industrial section of northeast Minneapolis for decades are giving way to microbreweries and taprooms, restaurants, and co-working spaces. Yet in the basement of an old dairy on Broadway Street, there's an organization of volunteers – Mobility Worldwide – that is transforming and saving lives around the world, one person a time. Most people take walking for granted, but there are over seventy million people in the world who are leg disabled. Birth defects, polio, injuries, landmines, disease, and other causes can lead to this disability. For those who are leg disabled and live in developing countries, many have to literally crawl in the dirt. Traditional wheelchairs don't work well where the roads are unimproved. When given the gift of mobility, lives are immediately changed for the better.

Mobility Worldwide's vision is to end immobility. They provide a rugged, three-wheeled, hand-powered cart with hauling capacity.

These carts are donated to people in developing countries who do not have use of their lower limbs. Developed in the late 1990s in response to a need identified in Africa, the carts are built in the US, but distributed exclusively overseas. There are twenty-three production sites in the US. Each cart costs roughly $300 to build and ship. Donations fund the cost of materials and shipping. The staff is all volunteer. Since 1994, over 78,000 mobility carts have been built and distributed in 106 countries using over 70 distribution partners.

In 2011, Jim Conn, a retired program manager from the aerospace industry, learned of Mobility Worldwide and the carts they provided the poorest of the poor. He was immediately hooked and became the director of the first affiliate in Minnesota.

Jim says, "Sometimes you ask how I, as one individual, can change the world? These carts change lives. The looks on the faces of recipients are ample evidence of that. Their testimony is further evidence. People everywhere can help change the world for the better. Without our help, they crawl in the dirt. These carts change their world. The carts provide much more than mobility; they offer freedom, dignity, and self-confidence."

Jim continues, "You see, in many societies, people with disabilities are shunned, avoided, and believed to be cursed. They are often not even acknowledged as people, which is cruel. When they get their carts, they gain self-respect and hope for a better future."

The volunteers of Mobility Worldwide are retirees, students, and groups from churches and community service organizations. After a short training and orientation, they provide the labor to assemble and package the carts. Working together in small teams, volunteers enjoy their experience at Mobility. They know they are making a difference. The Minnesota chapter just loaded a container – shipping its 1130th cart – to Nigeria.

Jim recalled his first distribution trip to Tanzania. "While everyone who receives a cart is grateful, there was one person in particular who stands out to me. A young man in his 20s, his body misshapen from birth defects, was carried on the back of his mother to the pickup site. His mother had carried him forty kilometers (nearly twenty-five miles) on her back. He received his cart and was ecstatic. For the first time in his life, he was able to get himself around. She didn't have to carry him. It was life changing for him – and for his mother, too."

Each cart has an area for storage and hauling. Most people use it to better themselves, whether it is to haul books and supplies to a school or to start a small business.

Jim spoke about a man in Kenya who had his cart for about fourteen months. When a volunteer saw him again, after the distribution, the cart – which is very sturdy and was designed to work with minimal maintenance for many years – was functional but pretty beat up. He asked the recipient why there was wear and tear. The Kenyan man said he used his cart to haul gold ore to the rock crusher. He loads a few hundred pounds of rock and takes it to the rock crusher in the hope of finding gold. People are very creative. Some will build canopies and use them as mobile vending machines or a mini food truck. Others will load the cart with a cooler and sell cold drinks. Jim recalled a man in Viet Nam who lost his legs to a landmine. With his new cart, he started a shoe repair business.

In Tanzania, after a woman received her cart, she went to the outskirts of town, tilled a garden, and planted and grew vegetables.

She harvested them and she took them back to town to sell. She is now self-sufficient economically. He recalls another woman who drove her cart to a local business with a knitting machine she could rent, so she could make clothes and then sell them at the market.

Jim's favorite story is about Seun Okoke, a beautiful young woman from Nigeria who was stricken with polio and scoliosis. She was leg disabled. With her cart and mobility, she was able to finish school and college. She's now working as an information technology specialist for the civil service.

Every day Seun rides the bus to work. She pays two fares, one for her and one for her cart. Then after work, she does the same to get back home.

Because she is able to work, she feels like she's a contributing member of society. Her self-esteem is high. She is now married and has a young son. Jim says Seun earns more than her husband, all due to the gift of her cart. She has been given the gifts of mobility and dignity that are immeasurable in value.[14]

Jim Conn's purpose: *To make a tangible difference in the lives of people around the world.*

Chapter 2: Set the Stage for Impact

What Defines Success?

To create great impact, there's an important question that you've got to answer. You are the only one who can answer it. The majority of people never ask, much less answer, this most important of questions. Instead, they drift through life.

Here's the question:

What is success to you?

This is a simple question of only five words. But if you've never thought about that question—and most people haven't—it's not so easy to answer.

If you know the answer, that's great! Write it down in your logbook. If you don't have the answer, here's an idea that may help you come up with your own.

Reflecting on the success question, it's useful to think about the eight key areas of life. Think of these eight key areas as the Wheel of Life.

In no particular order, they include: Health and Fitness, Family, Significant Other, Spiritual, Friends, Career, Financial, and Fun.

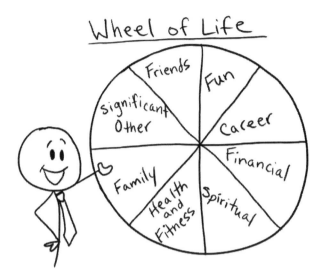

What's your current level of satisfaction today in each key area of life? How would you score yourself from a 1 (low) to 10 (high)? What's your current story in each area?

Next, pick a time in the near future, say three to five years, and pick the score of where you'd like to be for each key area of life. The difference between the current and future desired score represents the gap. For example, if in the financial area your current state is a 5, but you'd like to be able to score it a 10 in three years, then the gap is 5.

Why focus on three to five years? Because your definition of success will likely change as you enter new seasons of life. What success looks like to someone in their twenties and someone in their sixties is often quite different. So, that's why we focus on a shorter time horizon. You decide how many years it should be.

You'll want to come back to the question, *"What does success look like to me?"* every few years, at a minimum, as changes to life circumstances occur.

Now, after you've determined the gap between current and desired future states for each key area, answer this question:

What are the strategies you will need to deploy that will close the gap?

After you've scored each area for current and future states, and you have some strategies to close the gaps, think about your life overall.

It's useful to think at a high level about what success means to you overall in life. Look at your life from 35,000 feet, as though you were in a jet, looking down on your life. Reflect on these questions:

An ideal successful day looks like ...

I feel most successful when ...

Times in my past when I've felt successful are ...

Measurements of my success are ...

To feel like my life has been a success, I will need to accomplish ...

Everyone wants something different. For some, their health and fitness are far more important than their career. For others, being in an intimate, loving relationship with the right partner is far more important than being abundant financially. For others, their faith guides their life journey. If it came to a tradeoff between career and money and their faith, they would opt for faith every time. There are no right or wrong answers. It's what is most important to you. You'll need to do some soul searching to determine which of the key areas are truly most important to you and which are the less important areas.

Once you've done this, it's useful to write a few sentences that describe what success is to you. This is about answering the question:

"What do I want out of life?"

Defining success is to visualize the kind of life you seek and to know whether your life is on track. So, reflect on your answer to this statement carefully: "Success to me is…."

Some examples of "Success to me" statements include:

- Success to me is positively impacting the life of every person I meet.

- Success to me is finding and playing an important role in a business that takes great care of customers and team members. I wish to serve an important social cause and not harm the environment. I wish to recognize and appreciate all people. I want a role where I can grow and develop. Success is also having a close group of friends and finding a partner.

- Success to me is creating a movement that makes it unnecessary for anyone to feel lonely or isolated.

- Success to me is seeing everyone in the US having access to universal coverage for good healthcare.

- Success to me is to start up a business that serves a significant purpose and creates great value for customers, employees, and stakeholders. Success is to be rewarded for my work. Success is to stay in excellent physical shape and live a happy life with my close friends.

- Success to me is having enough money to provide a good home and to care for my family. Success is to stay in shape, to have a few close friends, and to continue to climb the corporate ladder so I can become a better provider down the road.

- Success to me is to raise my children to be strong, self-sufficient adults and to provide them with the best life possible that a single parent can offer.

- Success to me is to live a life of purpose, to have an impact, and to thrive. To grow deeper in my faith with my loving husband and to raise our children well, so they become responsible adults. Success means to nurture and experience rich relationships with friends and extended family. To give back and pay it forward as I can.

- Success to me is to live healthy while encouraging veganism to be accepted by family and friends. To make good tasting, healthy, and easily adopted food in order to reduce environmental damage and suffering to animals. I'll do this through peaceful and factual dialogue with everyone with whom I interact.

- Success to me is to have a healthy, happy, and loving retirement with my wife of thirty-five years, as we grow closer with God and prepare for our eternal life. To leave a legacy of memories, positive experiences, and life lessons to our children and grandchildren. Success means hearing, "Well done, faithful servant," when my time on this earth has come to an end.

- Success to me is traveling the world with friends, having fun, and passionately enjoying all that life has to offer.

Now it's your turn. As we move through the next sections of the book, it is vitally important for you to define success. Know yourself. Choose the right "yardstick" for measuring success in your life for the next ten years. If you don't decide, the world has a way of deciding for you. So once again, what do you want out of life?

Success to me is:

_____

_____

Success Is Creating Healing Retreats to Discover Peace and Purpose

It's beautiful to find an artist who creates only for the sake of art. One who feels wonder and serenity while creating his art.

If you are in northern New Mexico and hear a tap-tap-tap, it just might be Ra Paulette. Paulette is an American cave sculptor who lovingly and intentionally digs into and scrapes sandstone – solidified sand dunes, which were once the shores of an ancient sea – in order to transform the material into elaborate artistic spaces inside mountains.

For the past 25 years, with only his dog as company, he's been scraping and shaping the New Mexico sandstone into man-made art caves.

Working alone, he uses hand tools to do his work: picks, shovels, scrapers, mirrors, and a wheelbarrow. There is no dynamite, no drills, no sledgehammers, no generators, no power tools or conveniences of any kind. It's a grueling, arduous process and the manual labor is backbreaking.

Describing himself as "simply a man who has found his passion," Paulette is not an architect, he has no degree in sculpture, and he is not a structural engineer. He prepares no drawings or blueprints to guide his efforts. He calls himself an "intuitive engineer" and feels like an archaeologist, uncovering something that is already there by creating space through extraction.

Ra digs horizontally into a hill or mountain, about fifteen to twenty feet, and then he breaches the ground to open a hole on the top of the cave for sunlight. He can feel the empty space. And he digs and creates what he calls "the juxtaposition of opposites." You enjoy a sense of being underground with streaming light – it creates a perception trick. There is intimacy in being in a cave with high walls, with columns and arches sometimes 30 to 40 feet high. Light floods in.[15]

These wilderness shrines are massive in scale and poetic in design. He finishes the caves with scallops, molded curves, smooth ledges, inlaid stones, narrow pods, and crusty ledges. He wants his work to take your breath away in its magnificence.

He believes his work is magical. He's totally obsessed with cave sculpting. When he's engaged on a project, he thinks about it all day long. He dreams about his cave when he sleeps. He's passionate about his calling.

Ra doesn't do it for the money. Over the past 25 years, he's sculpted over a dozen caves, each about the size of a house. A project takes at least nine hundred hours, but it may take two years or more to complete. He charges about fifteen dollars per hour for the project. And now in his late sixties, he acknowledges he doesn't have much time to continue his art. His work was chronicled in *Cavedigger*, a documentary that was so unique it was nominated for an Academy Award.[16]

He describes his caves as celebrations that create transformative experiences. They are an aesthetic adventure. He seeks to open people's feelings. He views his caves as hallowed places and healing retreats. They are sanctuaries for prayer and meditation where transformations occur. He hopes that visitors to his sculpted caves will come in and find the solitude that he experiences. To find a sense of peace and purpose. To share a sacred moment when they can gain a deeper understanding of themselves and life.

Ra Paulette's gift: *His ability to visualize what could be and to create space from extraction.*

Ra's purpose: *To give others a deeper understanding of themselves.*

Committed to living an expressive life, Ra doesn't put any energy into being a success in the world. But he does put all of his energy and passion into living a life of purpose.

How does Ra define creating impact?

By creating healing retreats to discover peace and purpose.

Now that you've defined what success is to you, let's determine your unique gift so that you can use it to mine for and define your personal purpose.

What's Your Unique Gift?

Each of us — you, me, everyone — comes into this world with a unique gift. It's a personal characteristic you are endowed with, even if you don't know today exactly what that gift is.

If you are to create maximum impact with your life, it is imperative that you identify and apply your unique gift. When you decide to be a person of influence and impact, it's imperative that you help and encourage others to identify and apply their unique gifts, too.

35

"You have a one of a kind gift to offer this world, and you are unique in the entire history of creation." Wayne Dyer

The requirement for living a life of purpose and impact is to know and apply your gift. That's the pathway for a life of meaning and fulfillment. It is in the application of your gift for a purpose greater than you that allows you to impact others and make an impact on the world.

What is your unique gift?

If you don't know it yet, or just aren't sure, don't fear. I'll show you some steps to help you clarify that special gift. To find it requires some self-awareness and a willingness to do some self-discovery. Once you find it and accept it, you can refocus your life around that unique gift.

Your skills and strengths aren't your gifts. A skill is taking information you've learned or experienced and organizing this information into a series of steps that will lead to a desired performance. The information may be factual or something from which you've gained experience.

Taylor Davis is an American violinist, born in 1987. She started playing violin at the age of eight. She continued to play violin in college, majoring in public relations and minoring in violin performance. As a classically trained violinist, she had hoped to be a concert violinist, but those jobs are few and the competition is brutal. So she used her major and took a job in marketing and public relations in 2011. Still desiring to play violin, she decided to make YouTube videos on the side. In time, she caught the public's attention and her videos went viral. She records out of her home, and she uses a midi-board to produce her own scores. She has now posted over one hundred fifty videos and has over 200 million video views with one million subscribers. She tours and performs live events all around the world and her business is thriving.

What is Taylor's gift? What are her skills? What are her strengths? Clearly, she's been blessed with the gift of performing music. She's learned classical violin, which has allowed her to perform at a high level. So, that is her skill. Other skills she's developed are social media expertise, marketing expertise, and music production expertise. Her strengths include focus, adaptability, creativity and a high level of results-orientation. When the traditional avenue for performing didn't bear fruit, she didn't quit exercising her gift. She took advantage of the growth of YouTube and built her own brand. She didn't need a metropolitan orchestra to share her gift. Ironically, today she is playing in those same concert halls – the ones that were closed to her five years before – to sold out audiences. She applied her skills and strengths to her unique gift to create enormous impact.[17]

Using Taylor Davis as our example, can you see the difference between gifts, skills, and strengths?

For Taylor, her gift of performing music, applied creatively and diligently, created a direction for her life that unfolded literally before her eyes.

Reflect on your life. The events. The people. The opportunities that have come your way. When you reflect on your life at the proverbial altitude of 35,000 feet, you can gain a more panoramic view of the events of your life and your gift becomes clearer.

Unfortunately, most people don't do this type of reflection. Why? For several reasons:

1. They are too busy with busy-ness
   Perhaps they are so consumed with having a screen in front of them at all times, focusing on the lives of others and suffering from a fear of missing out, that they don't have the appetite or acknowledge the reflective work that would allow them to live a more purposeful, productive, and impactful life.

2. <u>They define themselves by a job title or a career</u>
   They don't look deeper and reflect deeper to explore their underlying unique gift.

3. <u>They minimize the idea that they have a unique gift</u>
   Everyone has a unique gift. It doesn't matter your age, income, or profession.

4. <u>They don't see the need – or have the desire – to do the self-discovery work</u>
   If you don't do the reflection, you won't find the gift. Isn't it worth it to put in a bit of effort to get to know yourself better to identify that unique gift? You can purposefully and intentionally apply that unique gift in life.

These reasons don't apply to you, right?

Let's see if we can get that unique gift identified by reflecting on these questions:

Who are you?

Describe yourself in just a few words. What descriptors would you use? Examples might include that you are a loving husband, an inspired saver of the earth, a passionate artist, a committed leader of others, a discoverer of new cures, a healer of the body and soul, a matriarch of the tribe, a body shaper, a loving image-shaper, a faithful friend, and so on. So, in just a few words, describe yourself.

What is it that people come to you for?

What are you naturally good at—so good that other people compliment you? When others consult you for advice, what do they ask you about? They may say, "You are so good at that!" And you may not even realize what you do and how you do it that makes this characteristic a special, unique gift. You may minimize the gift or even take it for granted. Or it may seem like everyone can do it, so you don't think twice about its uniqueness. When others come to you and ask, "How do you do that?" you can rest assured that it is a valuable gift. You find the gift comes naturally and you apply the gift unconsciously. What is your gift?

What would others miss?

Survey your close friends, work colleagues, and family members, and ask them, "What do you see as my three greatest gifts? And what would you miss if I were no longer here?" How would they respond? What do you think they would say? Write it down.

They may ask "Is there something wrong?" Or, "What's up with you?" as those are admittedly questions you don't get asked every day. So, when you ask, you'll want to start by sharing with them their greatest gifts, and what you would miss if they were no longer here. It's a wonderful way to demonstrate what that person means to you and your love for them. By sharing with them their gifts, you appreciate their uniqueness and honor them.

What do you do that feels effortless and gives you energy?

When you give your gift, it feels effortless. Far from expending your energy, the use of your gift renews your energy. You give it naturally to others, and you give it often. What is the gift?

Hopefully, you have several gifts that you've identified with one particular gift emerging as the one that is unique. Can you identify your number one unique gift?

If you are still struggling, request the input of others who are close to you. Others often have a clearer view of your special gifts.

Let me give you an example. I'm fortunate to be part of a small group of eleven men who meet each Saturday morning to lift up and encourage one another. Since we meet on Saturday mornings, we call ourselves the SAM Group. At our meetings, we check in with one another, talk about life's ups and down, the opportunities and challenges we face, and how we can help each other become better men. For more information about our group, you can check out the daily devotional book we co-authored, *Good Men, Great Thoughts: A Daily Devotional,* available at Amazon.[18]

A few years ago, we learned about a concept called the Round of Praise, where we shared with each other the top gifts we saw in each man and what we'd miss if he were no longer a part of the group. We shared this information on index cards. We had a week to prepare so we could give the exercise some serious thought.

When we next met, we delivered the cards to each member. While the members may have described each particular man's gifts using different words, it was easy to see there were common gifts that everyone saw in each man. After giving everyone a chance to read and absorb their precious input, we went around the room and each man shared a "What I Read" summary. This Round of Praise gave us an opportunity to elaborate, give examples, and share stories about the man being praised. It was a moving and joyful experience, with each participant gaining a clear understanding of the gifts he possessed, which the individual often took for granted, as seen by his close friends.

As a follow up to the Round of Praise, building on the gifts the men shared with one another, each man created a personal "unique gift" statement. As you gain clarity on your unique gift, can you create a gift statement that describes what you are called to do to apply your gift?

Here are a few examples:

- My gift is transparency and genuineness. I use my gift to help others, sharing my emotions and vulnerabilities to build trust and create a degree of calmness with those I meet.
- My gift is recognizing and focusing on what others do well, so I can help them apply both personally and professionally to optimize the impact of their gifts.
- Time and patience are my gifts, which I use to help those around me—family, friends, and strangers.
- As one who navigates and guides people down the river of life, I assist new widows as they transition from heartbreak and loss to a future of hope and possibility.

Now it's your turn.

Based on your reflections, what is your unique gift?

What is your unique gift statement?

Congratulations! You've now landed on your unique gift – the gifts that make you special, a one-of-a-kind. That's pretty awesome, isn't it? You bring a uniqueness that no one else in the world brings. Now, you know what it is.

As you've defined it, you get to apply your gift to the opportunities and situations that come your way. How will you apply your gift more often going forward, like Frank Pleticha applies his gifts of empathy, compassion, and active listening? Write down your response in your logbook.

How will you apply your gift more often in the future?

"Not on My Watch!"

Frank Pleticha, a marketing research manager at a financial services firm in Minneapolis, enjoyed his job, but he wouldn't have gone so far as to call it his purpose.

He had recently attended a seminar where the speaker challenged the attendees with what Frank described as a life-changing question: *"What gives you juice?"* At that time, Frank struggled to answer the question.

A few months later, a friend invited him to attend a human trafficking panel discussion at a local college. Frank described the event as a "complete eye-opener." While Frank had heard of sex trafficking in India and Thailand, he was shocked to hear how prevalent it was across the US. The convergence of major expressways and an international airport, combined with close proximity to the rural Upper Midwest and other factors, earned the Minneapolis-St. Paul metro area the dubious distinction of being one of the leading metropolitan areas in the US for sex trafficking.

Minneapolis Police Department Sergeant Grant Snyder's remarked, "Don't think sex trafficking is a problem in another part of town. It's taking place within two blocks from here. Right now. It's happening in your comfortable suburb where you live. And the kids who attend your junior high schools and high schools are being targeted. That's a fact and that's how insidious this problem is."

Frank learned that human trafficking is growing faster than any other criminal industry. That commercial sexual exploitation of children victimizes two million children globally. Additionally, this modern slavery has an annual revenue of $32 billion, exceeding the annual revenues of Major League Baseball, the National Basketball Association, the National Hockey League, and the National Football League – combined!

Frank volunteered for anti-trafficking training, attended more seminars and events, and watched documentaries such as *Nefarious: Merchants of Souls* and *The Whistleblower*. As he heard the pain of the victims, their sense of loss, their lack of self-esteem and hopelessness, their stories broke his heart. And learning the average age of those forced into prostitution in the US is thirteen, he was on fire. This revelation ignited Frank's passion to do something. He proclaimed, *"No, God! Not on my watch"* and he began to act.

He connected with Trafficking Justice, a Minnesota-based volunteer organization that shares facts about how people are exploited today. The organization brings hope and healing to victims. Frank learned that in order to slow the growth of sex trafficking, three audiences need to be addressed: victims, traffickers, and buyers.

Frank sees his purpose of eradicating this injustice in Minnesota similarly to how William Wilberforce, a British politician and a leader of the movement to abolish the slave trade in the 1800s, saw his mission. He borrowed Wilberforce's quote to British Parliament, when he speaks to others on the evil and pervasiveness of sex trafficking in Minnesota, the US, and world. "You may choose to look the other way, but you can never again say that you did not know."

Frank spoke to the pastoral team and members of his church, Grace Fellowship in Brooklyn Park, to build awareness. Through a series of events and sheer persistence, things began to move. Frank calls the shift similar to turning a giant, heavy flywheel. It takes a lot of effort to get it moving at all, but with persistent pushing in a consistent direction over a long enough period of time, the flywheel builds momentum, eventually hitting a point of breakthrough.

While Frank has been a catalyst, one person can't do it alone. He's building the team at Grace Fellowship and elsewhere to take a multi-faceted approach to addressing victims, traffickers and buyers. As Frank has mobilized his church's talent, time and financial resources to focus on this problem, he speaks of a future vision, ideally five to ten years out, when sex trafficking in Minnesota is discussed in the past tense.

Over the past few years, Frank's eyes have been opened to a world that he'd never seen. It's changed the course of his life. A man of deep faith, Frank firmly believes this crisis screams for a Christian response of compassion for the victims, justice for the buyers and traffickers, combined with redemption for all. His hope is to see a recovery ministry, with each service filled with people going through the recovery process and having hope for a better tomorrow.

Frank's goal is to bring hope to the victims and to end sex trafficking in Minnesota. He's not doing it for the fame and adoration. Even if no one knows his name, he yearns for the day when he hopes to hear Jesus Christ say, "Well done, my good and faithful servant."

The crisis of modern-day sex slavery doesn't need interested observers, it needs incurable fanatics. Frank is an incurable fanatic.[19]

Frank's gift statement: *Through my gift of empathetic and active listening, I help channel resources and contacts to the broken person sitting in front of me.*

Frank's purpose is: *Being a channel for those in broken situations to get connected to the Healer.*

The impact Frank is aiming for in a decade: *"To eradicate sex trafficking in Minnesota and beyond!"*

You can't sit back and wait for your gift to drop in your lap like a piano falling from the sky. You need to do the self-discovery. Your gift is the most important ingredient to defining your life's purpose. Applying that gift through purpose is like magic. It's your secret to making a great impact.

Chapter 3: Mine for Purpose

What's Your Purpose?

If you were asked by NBC News anchor Lester Holt, in front of a live audience of 12 million people, to describe your purpose in life – not a summary of your job description or your company's purpose – could you deliver it in a sentence or two with clarity and conviction?

If you answered "no" or "not sure," you've got plenty of company. It's been reported that 70% of leaders don't know their purpose.[20] That number is even higher in the general population.

Would you be led by someone who isn't clear about their purpose? What's the risk of being led by someone who isn't clear about his or her purpose? What if that person is you?

Maybe you've wrestled with these questions:
- What am I doing with my life?
- What is the meaning of my life?

- Am I living my truth?
- What is life asking of me?
- Am I making a difference?

Maybe with your work you feel like your job isn't a calling. You may be wondering if this is all there is.

- Or you're bored.
- Or you're exhausted and out of juice.
- Or you're feeling irrelevant.
- Or perhaps you feel trapped.
- Or maybe you are in a transition.
- Or you are restless and unsettled.
- Or perhaps you've had enough financial and material success, but there's no spiritual connection to your work.

These questions are all signals that it's time to get clarity of purpose. It's time to mine for and define your purpose. There is a purpose waiting for you that will engage your heart and head for your life.

What's the price you pay if you don't gain clarity of purpose?

Aristotle wrote of two kinds of happiness: hedonic and eudemonic. Hedonic happiness has to do with pleasure and having a good time. Eudemonic happiness is about feeling purpose and fulfillment. It's the second type of happiness that is the highest human good. If you feel meaning and purpose at work, you'll feel more eudemonic happiness. You'll perform better, be more passionate, and be more valuable.

"Happiness is the whole aim of human existence."
Aristotle

With no purpose, you'll likely chase pleasures or passions. What you are really looking for is your purpose. If you chase passion only, you won't feel purpose. You'll still feel empty. A purpose gives you clarity. It's a vision and it serves as a North Star for your life. An unfulfilled purpose infects you in many ways – ultimately to your peril.

Where there is no Vision, the people perish.

— Proverbs 29:18

The conundrum is this: where do you go to find your purpose?

Few think it's important to teach meaning or purpose. It's not taught in school. It's doubtful your parents taught you how to discover your purpose. Your company hasn't shown you how to find your purpose.

You can't find it on Google Maps. And that Smart TV with Ultra HD and 4K came with better instructions than anything that explains how to find purpose in your life.

There's good news. Your life purpose is inside of you, just waiting to be released. It's there! You've just got to find it. You'll need to mine for it. And I'll show you how to mine for purpose in this chapter.

You'll be introduced to Diana Pierce and Chris Bentley who've both mined for and discovered their purposes. They have designed their lives around their purposes and are flourishing on their respective journeys.

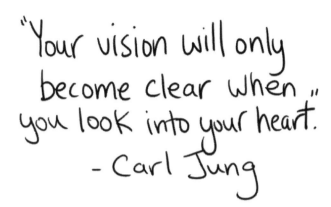

"Your vision will only
become clear when "
you look into your heart.
- Carl Jung

Your purpose doesn't have to be world changing or daunting like finding a vaccine for the Coronavirus. Your purpose can be simple. But it must be your essence.

Your purpose has existed within you for quite some time. When you closely reflect on your life using the purpose framing questions – which I'll invite you to do at the end of this chapter – there are "red threads of purpose" that have run through your life. Perhaps, until now, you have not fully recognized or appreciated these red threads. But as the years pass, these red threads become more refined and amplified.

Sharing Stories Where People Are Living Their Passion

For nearly thirty-three years in the Twin Cities, Diana Pierce was one of the most beloved and enduring television personalities. She has been a cornerstone of the region as a news anchor and reporter for the NBC KARE11 family. A hall-of-fame broadcaster, she retired from the airwaves in 2016. But she's as busy as ever, founding an online show entitled, "What's Next with Diana Pierce," where her passion is to help others tell their stories, moving hearts as well as minds.

"The germ of 'What's Next with Diana Pierce?' came from people stopping me at the grocery store and asking me, what's next for you?" the former anchorwoman said. "With what we're doing now, I want them to reflect on what's next for them, too." "What's Next?" is a Facebook Live broadcasted show that helps baby boomers discover new ideas for pursuing their passions and dreams as they approach their "what's next?"[21]

For the show, Diana books and interviews small-business owners and "encore career" entrepreneurs, financial planners, musicians, authors, and representatives of nonprofits started by or serving the older set. According to the Facebook metrics that Diana studies, "What's Next?" has a strong following with viewers between the ages of 40-70, with two-thirds of them women. Viewers can stream her weekly show at 7 p.m. most Thursdays via Facebook and watch more than 50 previously recorded segments on Facebook or YouTube.

Diana believes that "Stories define us. When we want someone to know us, we tell our stories. Given enough time with someone, we might discover similar themes that connect us. We want to share what is deeply true for us. We also want to share that mental thread that motivates us onward and reassures us that what we've been doing, when we're away from family and friends, makes sense when we endure hard work."

"I'm delivering original content that's interesting and inspiring to viewers who are 50-plus. I look for stories of people in that age group who are chasing their dreams," she said. Their lives are changing. They have energy and time and are engaging in new activities. Where will their passion lead them?"

Diana herself is modeling the very sort of personal reinvention that she advocates through her videocast. She's gone from anchor, with a supporting team of dozens of photojournalists, reporters and producers, to a do-it-yourself venture. Diana is on both sides of the camera and calls all the shots. She's using her gear to craft content delivered on a platform, not over the airwaves. She's watched on tablets and smartphones, not televisions.

Along with her business and life partner Scott Bemman, they produce the show together as it uploads to Facebook.

"This has had an immense learning curve for us. It's trial and error figuring the workarounds with rendering, streaming, and editing. These have not been my skills, but I now have the proficiency to get the job done. I'm in this new arena with people in their 20s and 30s. No one my age is creating a product this way," Diana said.

"Broadcasters haven't typically served the 50-plus viewer, but this is a group of people with expendable income (that) they're happy to spend."

It's my hope that when you see people sharing their story on "What's Next with Diana Pierce," that you will reflect on what's true for you and that it could possibly result in a life change, whether it's big or small, in your story of "What's Next."[22]

These days Diana is intensely interested in passion – her own and that of other Minnesotans in midlife and beyond. She's blazing new trails with her venture and is inspiring, educating, and creating great impact for baby boomers as they enter their next phase. Her impact is educating and encouraging those who are 50+.

Diana Pierce's purpose: *Creating content for the 50+ crowd and sharing stories of people living their passion.*

The Forward Pointing Arrow

Purpose is the overarching guiding principle that gives your life meaning.

Purpose is a forward-pointing arrow. When you are clear about your life purpose, with an explicit, written purpose statement, you will know why you get out of bed in the morning. It incorporates your special gifts and life experiences. When you write and share your purpose story, not only will others know and trust you, chances are they'll be inspired to write and share theirs, too. With the material you are discovering in this book, you can guide them through this process.

Purpose is your unique definitive statement about the difference you are trying to make in the world. It's your aim or direction. Simply put, your purpose is to discover and live your life purpose. It's what gives life meaning. Purpose enables you to thrive.

Opportunities come your way in life. By applying your unique gift to these opportunities, you discover your purpose. But you can't just sit still and wait for it to drop into your lap. You've got to do the self-discovery work.

> *"The one who created you without you, will not confirm you without you."*
> Augustine

The pursuit of purpose is biological. It's built into your DNA. Your brain has a "seeking system" that encourages you to explore, learn, and find meaning. Your brain is wired to want to know, understand, and experience your purpose and positive emotions. You're wired to be simultaneously driven toward something and pulled to it. It's an innate desire to understand and make meaning. So, defining your purpose is a need that humans share with one another.

To make purpose resonate, it's important that it serves a cause bigger than you. You can create a lot of meaning in your own life by helping someone else do something that is meaningful to them.

"The best way to find yourself is to serve others."

– Gandhi

Your purpose may have nothing to do with what you do for a living. Your career may not be your calling. While you may get fired from your job, you can never be fired from your purpose. If you can get fired from it, you haven't discovered your purpose yet. Your purpose is not about the expertise you bring your job, either. Let's not make our position or expertise our purpose.

For it to be your purpose, it must work in all areas of your life.

Mining for and discovering your purpose mean embracing your gifts, capturing your essence, and living authentically. When you are clear about your purpose, you'll never feel like you are an impostor.

Your purpose is unique to you. It can do no harm. It permeates all areas of life. While your purpose may change with life's seasons, the "red thread" of purpose never changes in your life.

When you are living by purpose, everything seems natural. It may not be easy, but you must live authentically. In your sweet spot. It's like a baseball hitter or golfer who hits the ball on the sweet spot. Living on purpose is like the ball hitting the bat on the sweet spot. It just flies effortlessly.

When you've defined your purpose statement and live by purpose, there are many benefits. It serves as a filter. When an opportunity or experience presents itself, you ask, "Does this situation help me fulfill my purpose?" Or, "If I say yes to this experience, is that consistent with my purpose." It allows you to quickly and definitively answer "Yes" or "No." "Is what I'm about to do in keeping with my purpose and values?"

Viktor Frankl, author of *Man's Search for Meaning*, founder of logotherapy, and a concentration camp survivor, wrote "Man's search for meaning [purpose] is the primary motivation in life. [Defining your purpose is] the most important activity for your development. With it, we can survive even the worst conditions. It gives us meaning in life."[23]

The imperative of logotherapy is: "Live as if you were living already for the second time and as if you had acted the first time as wrongly as you are about to act now!"

> *"Man's main concern is not to gain pleasure or to avoid pain, but rather to seek a meaning [purpose] in his life."*
> Viktor Frankl

Frankl suggested you can discover this meaning (purpose) in life in three different ways:
- By creating a work or doing a deed;
- By experiencing something – nature and culture – or encountering someone or something – goodness, truth, beauty, and love; and
- By the attitude we take toward unavoidable suffering.

Purpose isn't the same as passion. Purpose doesn't change. Passions change. What you were passionate about at the age of eight, 18 or 28 may not be something you are passionate about today. Think about things – or people – you've loved before, but no longer do. You were passionate then, but not now.

If you work for a highly purpose-driven organization, don't mistake the group's purpose for yours. As an example, there are many who work in purpose-driven world health organizations that have a crisis of meaning in their personal lives when one child is healed while others around them die. That causes one to question whether they are really making a difference. And meaning can be elusive. So, while it is great to work in purposeful companies whose purpose resonates for you, the organization's purpose is not your life purpose. Be careful not to fall into that trap.

Perhaps the biggest reason people have difficulty in believing that life has a purpose is because they do not see themselves as deserving or important enough to have a purpose. They may think it is too bold. They've settled to play small. That limiting belief will hold you back. It's inaccurate thinking, too.

Think about Rosa Parks. She was an unknown seamstress in a department store in Montgomery, Alabama, until December 1, 1955, when she defied an order by a white bus driver to relinquish her seat in the "colored section" to a white passenger, when the "whites only" section was filled. Parks was "tired of giving in" and became an international icon for resistance to racial segregation. Rosa Parks didn't have a powerful job, but she had a powerful purpose. Rosa Parks was an ordinary person – just like you and me.

"There is no passion to be found in playing small—Settling for a life that is less than the one you are capable of living."
—Nelson Mandela

Heeding your purpose isn't an easy path, which is why most people never know it. They don't listen to their hearts. Or if they do and follow their calling, they fear the unknown, and they fear looking foolish or failing. So, they play it safe and drift along. Perhaps they are comfortable. Perhaps they have the means, but they lack the meaning. And they never create the impact they were born to make. Don't let this be you.

"Would it not be better to ask people to what purpose are they applying their life, rather than simply asking them what they do for a living?" Thom Winninger, author, *Your True DNA!*

It's time to go mine for purpose. Pull out your logbook and thoughtfully answer the following purpose framing questions. The outcomes will be the raw material for your purpose statement and story.

When you were young, what activity brought you the most happiness and satisfaction? What were the specifics? What emotions do you feel as you recall these memories?
Hint: It could be one specific moment, a specific activity, or a list of experiences.

What have been the three most salient events in your life that have made you the person you are? Write one sentence that describes the gist of these events or experiences.

Hints: These are likely your most challenging life experiences. Pick an experience that is currently not impacting you.

Now, which of the three events would you call the single most defining moment in your life?
Hint: It is often – but not always – an event that happened early in life, often between ages 9-12, when you didn't have the answers for the challenges you faced.

Why do you get up in the morning?
Hints: What gets your blood flowing? What causes do you care about most deeply? What is a problem that "someone needs to fix"? What are you committed to that is bigger than you?

What are your three inviolable values?
Hints: What are the top three values that guide you? What are the values you could credibly have printed on a t-shirt to wear? People would agree, "Yes, that defines what you stand for and how you operate."

Using your unique gift and the responses to the purpose framing questions as raw material, reflect on the key words and phrases that jump out at you. Highlight the key words and themes. Can you see a pattern? A pattern – the gifts, the values, the red threads, the purpose – should begin to emerge.

It's time to create a purpose statement. Your purpose statement does the following:

1. Identifies the unique gift(s) you bring to the world;
2. Taps into your own life experiences (challenging times, passions, and best memories);
3. Uses a minimal number of words or symbols;

4. Consists of words that have deep meaning; and
5. Every time you recall and share your purpose, it provides clarity and focus to live on purpose.

Smarter people than your author recommend you meditate and contemplate intensively and extensively about your purpose statement. I suggest you do this, too.

Reflect on and complete this sentence:

"The purpose that is leading me is: _____."

Now edit your sentence into your purpose statement. Here are some examples.

To provide safe passage down the river of life, helping others to experience adventure, find and feel joy, and live life fully.

To show others that their daily marathons are possible to get through and that nothing is really impossible.

To help others look and feel great, and to lift up their happiness, confidence, and self-image.

Creating content for the 50+ crowd and sharing stories of people living their passion.

To be a channel for those in broken situations to get connected to the Healer.

To guide others through the moguls – so they see what is possible and become unstoppable.

To courageously dig deep to unleash potential as powerful as Nature.

What's the Story Behind Your Purpose?

Write and prepare to tell the story about your purpose. What's the story behind your purpose? How did you decide on your purpose statement? Tell us the story.

What are the keywords of your purpose statement? Why did you choose those words? How does it all fit together?

When you tell your purpose story to those close to you, you strengthen your bond with them. You encourage and inspire them to mine for their purposes and to write and tell their purpose stories. You'll lift their hearts with your story.

Authentic stories are powerful and can be used for many purposes. In today's world, with so much information flying at you from so many directions, you forget facts, figures, numbers and trends in the information overload. It's hard to sort out what is real, what is important, and what isn't. Information in the form of facts, figures, percentages, and statistical variances is directed to your head. It literally goes in one ear and out the other.

Your story, on the other hand, comes from the heart and is directed to the heart. People will remember it forever and want to hear it again and again. It will move them. To influence and persuade, you aim for the heart and then the head.

Your story is the connective tissue that draws others to you. It tells how you overcame adversity, and how that experience is relevant today and tomorrow.

Your story helps others understand what is important to you, how your life experiences have made you what you are today and why you do what you do.

Sharing your purpose story is the most generous thing you can do when you tell it with conviction and authenticity, you'll hold your audience's attention like a magnet.

"Those who tell the stories rule society."
– Plato

Your author's "Who am I" story, titled *"The Game of Catch,"* appears in the book *The Reinvented Leader: Five Critical Steps to Becoming Your Best*.[24] It can also be found in Appendix 5. Later in this book, in the *Pull It All Together* chapter, I'll invite you to write your "impact story," which includes your purpose statement, gifts, and impact declaration. My impact story, *"Encourage Others to Create Impact, One Person at a Time,"* is included in that chapter.

Let's read the inspiring story of Chris Bentley and see how he's discovered his purpose after age sixty.

Providing Safe Passage Down the River of Life

By all accounts, Chris is a happy, accomplished, and successful man. He knows where he's going and where he's been. Blessed with a strong faith, a beautiful wife and family, a thriving business, a close network of friends and good health, life is good. Chris lives purposefully and with passion, creating a positive impact for many.

He makes the world a better place. He operates with great clarity and is deeply fulfilled. He is at peace with his past. But it wasn't always this way. Here's Chris's story.

As the first-born child of a 19-year-old mother and a 29-year-old father, Chris remembers his childhood vividly. Now in his early 60s, he recalls how he continually sought affection and affirmation from his father while growing up.

Chris's father was a stoic workaholic from the Bay Area. When Chris was young, his father moved the family to Grants Pass, Oregon, his dad went to work at a small Savings and Loan bank. Chris refers to his father as "emotionally stoic." His dad wasn't physically abusive, but he was emotionally abusive and never expressed pleasure in any of Chris's actions, activities, or accomplishments. While his mom loved and quietly encouraged Chris, she too, desperately sought her husband's approval and affection and was careful to not anger him.

As a boy and young man, Chris hoped through hard work and perfection, he would eventually earn the love of his dad. He pushed himself relentlessly. In high school, Chris excelled academically, made National Honor Society, and worked side jobs. He was an all-conference football player, an expert skier and student body president.

A few years after their move to Oregon, Chris' father started Orange Torpedo Trips. During the summers, Chris served as a guide on the Rogue River in southern Oregon. As a guide, he safely led novice paddlers for nearly a decade, paddling over 10,000 miles of whitewater.

His senior year, Chris was recognized as the Jaycee's Student of the Year and received scholarships to Oregon State and the United States Naval Academy. Unfortunately, despite the many achievements, there were no acknowledgements or compliments from his dad.

At the Naval Academy, Chris placed in the top 10% of his class, lettered in boxing and was selected as a company commander. His father never visited him, never called, and never wrote. After graduation, for the first time in four years, his father visited Chris at the Academy, but there was no "Congratulations, son. Well done. I'm proud of you. I love you."

Following graduation and flight training, Chris was assigned to a P3 Orion "sub hunter" squadron to hunt Soviet submarines. As a Naval Flight Officer, Chris and his crew of 13 pursued Soviet submarines in the oceans of the world. As Mission Commander, Chris made sure his crew arrived back to base safely.

After the Cold War ended and after fourteen years of service, Chris took leave from the military and entered the private sector.

For the first forty years of life, Chris realized he strived – to no avail – to make his father proud. He worked extremely hard, was disciplined, goal-oriented, and persistent. His motto was "Failure is not an option." Yet, as focused and as hard as he tried to win his dad's love, he never succeeded. As Chris recalls, "My dad never delighted in me."

Some years later, his dad passed away. He and Chris had been estranged for twenty years.

Now, Chris is an accomplished and recognized financial advisor. Today he helps investors navigate up and down markets, avoid financial potholes, sail through recessions and arrive at retirement safely.

When Chris's colleague Dave unexpectedly and suddenly passed away, Chris assisted Dave's widow, Liane, to get her affairs in order.

As Chris worked with Liane, he recognized widows need help managing through the financial shocks of early widowhood, because couples often divide responsibilities and the widow doesn't always have the knowledge or wherewithal to tackle alone what was once a dual effort.

Chris learned that in widows' most vulnerable of times, they may not have anyone to help them with the practical issues of maintaining a home. Perhaps their husbands handled the financial affairs and managed the investments, so they are uninformed. Or they don't want to rely on family members for help. In a time of grief, suddenly the widow is faced with overwhelming decisions. She is simply unprepared.

As Chris did more research, he found that while there were many books available to widows, there was no organization that provided widows with timely financial and legal guidance at no cost.

Recognizing the need, he offered to address it with some of Liane's new friends from a widow's support group. The widows were extremely grateful for Chris's guidance and interest. From this experience, he felt called to do more.

Chris founded Wings for Widows, a public 501(c)(3) non-profit, that utilizes "angel teams" comprised of a financial professional and an experienced widow. After a comprehensive assessment of the widow's situation, they provide the widow guidance to address her financial and legal needs.

Wings for Widows offers a gentle hand to ensure new widows don't face a dark and taxing time of life alone. With plans to grow Wings for Widows far beyond Minnesota, Chris has found his purpose and has taken hold of a very big dream.

Looking back on his life and reflecting, Chris's "red thread" of purpose – the theme that runs through his life – was suddenly apparent. It is to provide safe passage for others. He's written his purpose statement and purpose story, which he's allowed me to share.

"As a young man, I was a river guide – helping our guests navigate more than 40 miles of whitewater. I provided safe passage from the put-in to the take-out.

As a naval officer, I was a Mission Commander – getting my crew to station, prosecuting enemy submarines, and returning home after 10-hour missions. I provided safe passage from take-off to landing.

As a sailor, whether skipper or crewman – I weathered storms topside, at the helm, day and night, ensuring safe passage of our sailing vessel and the passengers entrusted to my care.

As a financial advisor, I guide clients through up and down markets to help them retire comfortably and realize their dreams. I provide safe passage during a lifetime of living and investing.

As the founder of Wings for Widows, I provide safe passage for new widows, from heartbreak and loss to a future of hope and possibility.

The purpose, then, that seems to define me is:

To provide safe passage down the river of life, helping others to experience adventure, find and feel joy, and live life fully.

The impact Chris seeks to make: *"To make certain no new widow has to go it alone."*[25]

Now it is your turn to write and share your purpose story.

Will you write yours so that you can stay inspired and motivated to live on purpose?

Who needs to hear your purpose story?

Will you share your story and encourage others how to do the same?

If you need more on writing and telling your story, see pages of 67-72 of the book, *The Reinvented Me: Five Steps to Happiness in a Crazy Busy World.*[26]

"I apply my knowledge of the purpose of my life every day. It's the single most useful thing I've ever learned." Clayton Christensen, late professor at Harvard Business School and bestselling author

Chapter 4: Ignite Your Passions

If we met at Starbucks, started a conversation, and began discussing passion, could you quickly name your top three?

If these passions didn't fly off the tip of your tongue, I've found you'd be among the majority of people.

So let's get clear on your passions.

Even if you know your passions, are you tapping into them as a propellant for your purpose and in living a life of impact?

If not, that's unfortunate. Because passion is jet fuel for your purpose and for living a rich life. It's also the second critical ingredient needed to reinvent your impact.

If you find yourself not so passionate today, it didn't always used to be this way. You've been passionate in the past – even if you aren't today. When you were a child, you greeted new experiences with passion. You pursued activities you loved with zest.

"Nothing great in the world has ever been accomplished without passion."
George Hegel, German Philosopher

Gordon MacKenzie, the creative paragon at Hallmark Cards, reported his findings from the creativity workshops he held at elementary schools in his book *Orbiting the Giant Hairball*. MacKenzie levels an indictment: "From cradle to grave, the pressure is on: be normal."

When hosting creativity workshops, MacKenzie would conduct informal surveys by asking, "How many artists are there in the room?" In the first grade the entire class waved their arms like crazy.

In the second grade about half the hands went up. In the third grade a third of the kids responded. And by the time he got to the sixth graders, only one or two kids raised their hands, tentatively.

According to MacKenzie every school he visited was participating in suppressing creative genius by training kids away from their passions. Instead of passion being celebrated and validated, it was criticized. The voice of normalcy became the loudest voice in the room.[27]

Now, distracted with getting through the day, and perhaps getting kicked in the teeth by life, too many adults don't stop to think about what they are passionate about, or could be passionate about. So, they grind away. And that is a pity.

When asked to name passions, most don't answer with passions about their work. In a Canadian study about passion, 96% described their passions were about sports, nature, and the arts. Only 4% identified passions that had any relation to work or education.

In another recent study, Deloitte reported 88% of employees don't have passion for their work, so they don't contribute their full potential. Even worse, 80% of senior managers aren't passionate about their work! With senior leaders setting a poor example, is it any wonder that team members don't have passion for their work? But you can and must be different.[28]

Think talent is more important than passion? Which is more important when it comes to professional success? You might think it is talent, but an eleven-year study led by Dr. Daniel Heller would argue otherwise. The study surveyed 450 elite musical students and found that, over time, passion trumps talent. It was the students' passion for music that inspired greater risks and gave them the intrinsic motivation to persist in the face of adversity. At the end of the day, passion wins.[29]

Clearly, there's a passion problem today. If you seek to have a great impact, you'll need to get passionate about your purpose and work.

And that's the focus of this chapter. I'm going to show you three ways you can ignite your passions so you can gain more juice from your work and zest for your life. I'll get to that in a minute.

Engagement is Not Passion

First, let me clear up a myth about passion. There is too much time and attention given by organizations and leadership to something that is most definitely not passion. When we talk about the weak, passive, distant cousin of passion – that's employee engagement – we do our people and our organizations a disservice. You can be engaged and not passionate.

Passion isn't engagement.

Despite nearly $1 billion spent annually in the US on employee engagement, the percentage of workers who are engaged stays troublingly low – around one-third of the workforce – and that percentage has been more or less steady since Gallup began tracking engagement nearly 20 ago.

Getting employees engaged is typically a short-term effort and speaks to the extrinsic motivators that push people to "get into it" for a period of time. These extrinsic motivators include praise, incentives, conditions, and special events. Engagement is short-term and is focused on driving a performance bump.

Daniel Pink warns us in *Drive: The Surprising Truth About What Motivates Us*, about "the counterintuitive consequences of extrinsic incentives as 'the hidden costs of rewards.'" He cites "7 Deadly Flaws of Carrots and Sticks (extrinsic rewards): (1) They can extinguish intrinsic motivation; (2) They can diminish performance; (3) They can crush creativity; (4) They can crowd out good behavior; (5) They can encourage cheating, shortcuts, and unethical behavior; (6) They can become addictive; (7) They can foster short-term thinking."[30]

Passion is about identifying the longer-term intrinsic motivators to inspire you to work at a higher level. Like purpose. As you define purpose, what passions can serve as jet fuel to propel the purpose? Passionate people create great value. Passionate people strive for mastery.

So, we must set the bar higher. Engagement is insufficient. It's satisfactory underperformance. Let's shoot for a loftier target. We're going for passion. Because if you're passionate about life and work, you sure as heck are engaged! And when you are purposeful and passionate about life and work, committed to making an impact, you can do and create great things. When a team of purposeful and passionate team members are connected together, watch out!

Look at successful entrepreneurs. They are passionate about their purpose, a purpose that is deeper and more meaningful than the product or service alone.

When Doug Leone, the legendary investor from the venture capital firm, Sequoia Capital (the VC firm that backed Google, Airbnb, WhatsApp, and hundreds of other companies) was asked, "What is the one quality all of the successful entrepreneurs share?" He answered, "They don't do it for the money. They're passionate about their purpose."

"Their (company's) purpose might be to disrupt a category (Uber, Airbnb). Their purpose might be to solve a problem they faced themselves (WhatsApp). Their purpose might be to leave the world a better place."

Think of Howard Schultz of Starbucks. He says, "Coffee is the product, but it's not the business we're in." What Schultz is passionate about isn't coffee. Anyone can sell a cup of coffee. What he is passionate about is "creating a third place between work and home." It's about the experience Starbucks offers. Schultz' purpose is, *"To inspire and encourage the human spirit."*

The late Apple co-founder and CEO Steve Jobs told us, "People with passion can change the world."[31]

When Jobs returned to Apple in 1997 after a 12-year absence, he said, "Apple is not about making boxes for people to get their jobs done, although we do that well. Apple is about something more. Its core value is that we believe that people with passion can change the world for the better."

As we know, Apple revolutionized the personal computing, digital publishing, music, retail, smartphones, and tablet industries.

British Prime Minister Benjamin Disraeli, a man who helped shape the world stage in the nineteenth century, believed that "Man is only great when he acts from passion."

Everyone has had passions. Do you still have passions? Sometimes when you grind, you may be in a rut or slump, and you may feel "passionless." Your passions often change over time. Think about someone – or something – you might have felt passionate toward years ago but no longer feel passionate about today.

Attaching passion to your purpose, supported by your world-class productivity routine (which you'll read more about later in the book), will ensure that you'll make a great impact.

You don't have to be an entrepreneur, celebrity, or a high-powered corporate executive to operate with great purpose, passion, productivity or to create great value and impact for others. Alli Swanson isn't any of those, but she operates with purpose and great passion, creating an impact every day.

The Loving Image Shaper

As a young girl, Alli was the gregarious and outgoing one. Her older sister by 17 months always sent Alli ahead to meet new friends and try new experiences. It seemed everyone she came into contact with became a friend.

She had a natural gift for making friends. Perhaps it was because she started out by liking and being genuinely curious about them.

Her friends describe her as fun-loving, empathetic, caring, kind, patient, generous, an excellent listener, and a trusted friend.

In middle school, she enjoyed braiding her sister's and friends' hair and then trying out new hairstyles. They loved it when she made them look beautiful. Then came the makeup, nail polish and hair color. Alli joyfully assisted everyone in her circle to look their best. Her services were in high demand.

The bathroom she shared with her sister looked like the work sink and mixing station at a beauty parlor! And it smelled like a laboratory! But one thing was clear to Alli, she loved helping others look beautiful and she was passionate about making a bigger impact with her talents.

After graduation from high school, she chose the Aveda Institute for cosmetology training. The purpose of Aveda resonated with Alli and her values: "To care for the world we live in. To strive to set an example for environmental leadership and responsibility, not just in the world of beauty, but around the world."

She was a natural. A quick study. She rapidly developed her skills, and she committed to becoming her best for her clients. She excelled at Aveda and following graduation she quickly built up a loyal clientele at a salon in the trendy 50th and France shopping district of Edina, a Minneapolis suburb.

In a fast-paced, crazy-busy, turbulent, and distracted world, Alli welcomes her clients with a kind word, a smile, a caring and empathetic ear, a healing touch and an ability to make time slow down. A momentary oasis from the chaotic day-to-day grind. With love and great skill, in an hour or two, Alli brings out her customers' pure essence and makes them look and feel beautiful. In addition to a great hairstyle, Alli captures the hearts of her clients, connects with their minds, and bolsters their self-esteem. Alli loves making others feel beautiful, creating lasting friendships along the way. She is unique. She is passionate about being a loving image shaper.

Alli's purpose: *Helping others look and feel great, and uplift their happiness, confidence, and self-image.*

Alli's calendar fills up months in advance. For years, she's been voted by her clients as the "Best Hairstylist" in Edina Magazine's *Best of Edina* annual survey.

You find meaning when your actions reflect what you value, what is important to you, and what gifts you enjoy and want to give. Your gifts, values, and passions can guide you toward your purpose. You just have to commit. Just like Alli Swanson.[32]

When you're passionate about your purpose, you bring more energy to work. You become more resourceful in finding solutions to challenging problems and opportunities. You are happier at work. You perform at a higher level. You inspire others to become more passionate because passion is contagious. You create greater value for your stakeholders.

Do you have the passion to make an impact? Would you like to have the passion to make a bigger impact? Read on.

Passion is an inside job. It starts with you.

Time to pull out your logbook and answer the following question:

What needs to happen for you to operate with greater passion?

Some say, "Just follow your passions." I know, you've read it or heard it a million times. All the articles and commencement speeches suggest, "Just follow your passion." Is that good advice? Or not?

Do What You Love
and Follow your Passions.

Good advice? Or not?

For those who know exactly what they want to do in life, perhaps that is good advice. If you've been so passionate about chess that you must become a grandmaster, or if you've always yearned to be a surgeon, or a musician, or a professional athlete, then that counsel may be helpful.

But for most people, that advice is limiting. Most people haven't always known what they're going to do with their lives.

There is a better way to get more passionate about your purpose and work. There are three approaches to help you ignite your passions.

3 Steps to Passion

1. Make an Inventory;
2. Try New Things; and
3. Make a Commitment and Allow Passion to Follow.

Let's work on your passions. Let's inventory current and past passions. Then, you'll consider potential new passions. Finally, I'll invite you to make a commitment – and you can watch your passion follow. Let's see how this works.

Step 1: Make an Inventory

Sometimes in life, you forget about what once made you passionate. Let's look back at your life and create a list of what used to make your heart beat faster and blood race. Reflect on the following questions and write your responses in your logbook.

What have you been passionate about?

What are your top strengths?

What makes you energized and inspired?

What particular personality traits or strengths do you like to express?

If you are struggling with identifying your top strengths, consider taking some online assessments that will help you zero in on your strengths. Here are two that work well:

VIA Survey of Character Strengths focuses on your best qualities. It has been taken by over one million people. It's free.[33]

StrenghtsFinder identifies your top five strengths and has been taken by over 20 million people. It's called Gallup's *Clifton StrengthsFinder* and costs $19.95.[34]

Reflecting on your life, what activities, hobbies, and interests have stayed with you over time and why?
Hint: You don't have to be good at them, you just need to love doing them. How does participating in these activities make you feel?

What topics could you listen to hundreds of podcasts about and/or read hundreds of books about and not get bored?

What would you spend your time doing if you had complete financial abundance to do anything?

What are you here for? What do you love?

What are you against? What do you hate?
Hint: Issues or topics that cause you to react with emotion are good indicators of where your passions may lie.

What would you be doing if you jumped out of bed in the morning, excited to fulfill your purpose?

What are your superpowers?
Hint: It's not just superheroes who possess superpowers. You and I possess them, too. Howard Gardner shows us how to discover them.

In his classic book, *Frames of Mind*, Gardner, a professor of education at Harvard University, identified eight different modalities of intelligence. Each is possessed by every individual to a greater or lesser extent.

Amassing a wealth of evidence, Gardner identifies the existence of eight different intelligences, each as important as the next, that comprise a unique cognitive profile for each person. Think of these intelligences as superpowers.[35]

1. Linguistic intelligence
This is being word-smart and applying verbal skills smoothly. Professions: author, speaker, politician.

2. Logical and mathematical intelligence
Excellent numerical and reasoning skills. Professions: auditor, accountant, statistician, financial analyst.

3. Spatial intelligence
You are picture-smart. Deductive about space and objects. Profession: artist, graphic design, architect, engineer, photographer, pilot.

4. Body-Kinesthetic
About being body-smart. Physically proficient. Combination of body and mind. Perfect control of moves. Professions: athlete, dancer, actor, doctor, forest ranger.

5. Music intelligence
Skilled at ear and pitch, tone, and melody. Professions: musician, choral director, musical therapist, music teacher.

6. Interpersonal
Highly emotionally intelligent and people-smart. Astute at verbal and nonverbal communication. Self-awareness, empathy, sensitivity. Professions: sales, psychology, teacher, social director.

7. Intrapersonal intelligence.
Being self-smart and understanding self in a profound way. Professions: psychologist, coach, theologian, planner, entrepreneur.

8. Naturalist intelligence.
Understanding patterns in nature. Clear idea of manmade and natural developments. Professions: botanist, geologist, chef, meteorologist, landscaper.

Each of the intelligences have hundreds of applications.

Which superpowers do you possess in more abundance than others? Which sound like you? Rank them in order of dominance for you.

Now you have a lot of raw material about your strengths, talents and passions. Sorting through your reflections and findings, what does this information reveal about you and your passions? What are the themes? List your top three passions.

List Your Top Three Passions

1.
2.
3.

To what extent are you tapping into these passions? How could you let more of your passions flow?

Step 2: Try New Things

Dr. Carol Dweck introduced the concept of "growth mindset." She found that people are more likely to thrive when they believe their basic abilities can be developed through dedication and hard work. Her research has led to major advances in adult learning and an appreciation for the power of mindset in impacting behavior.[36]

Do you have a fixed or growth mindset?

People with a fixed mindset believe their qualities, personalities, strengths and weaknesses are set at an early age. Either you're good at something, or bad. People with a fixed mindset don't enjoy learning. They hit a brick wall. They believe "you can't teach an old dog new tricks."

People with a growth mindset believe a person's full potential is unknowable. They know that with training and commitment people can build new talents and capabilities. To thrive and create impact, you need a growth mindset.

To become more passionate, try new stuff and learn new skills. You weren't born to do one thing. You can do many things. Try some new, interesting things.

Why don't people try new things? Fear. What are the benefits of trying new things? You learn more about yourself. Your creativity gets stimulated. It makes you more interesting. It may even increase your marketability and make you more valuable.

What are new things you could try? You could try a new sport like wakeboarding, snowboarding, rock climbing, or maybe paddle tennis. What about cooking at home for a week with your partner? Try not going out to eat for a week. You can try new recipes. Or you can check out a new cooking theme, like Pete Evans who shows on Netflix how to prepare quick, flavorful, paleo meals for healthy eating.

Try new restaurants. Commit to trying out one new restaurant per month. Or, flip your interests for a month or so. If you like to go to sporting events, go to a play or a concert. Say "Yes" when you have opportunities to try new experiences and challenges.

Eric Barker, bestselling author of *Barking Up the Wrong Tree: The Surprising Science Behind Why Everything You Know About Success Is (Mostly) Wrong*, recommends "making small bets."[37] Try a short class or seminar, a trip to somewhere new, or a few hours of volunteering. Go out and experience a new restaurant, or take up a new sport, etc. Try these things to determine if you can get passionate about a new topic. So, what new passions could you potentially develop?

Put aside your fears, adopt a growth mindset and try something new. Put a small bet on it and see what happens!

Passions aren't fixed. They ensue.

Let's go back to that well-meaning but limiting statement: "Just follow your passion."

Simply "following" your passions can cause you to limit new things, new opportunities, and new fields. It may encourage you to give up when you encounter an obstacle or challenge.

Following your passion is well intended – but it's perhaps not the best advice. A 2018 study conducted at Stanford University found that interests can be "found" by trying new things.[38] The advice, "follow your passion," may actually make people less successful since it unrealistically implies an easy path to success and narrows your focus too much. It assumes you have a pre-existing passion waiting to be discovered.

The researchers found that "following your passion" comes with hidden implications. When you learn of a new interest, one that resonates for you, you may have an assumption that pursuing and mastering it will be easy. Once the challenges hit, this type of belief makes it likely you'll quit. People can discount an interest when it becomes too challenging.

The idea that passions are found fully formed implies the number of interests a person has is limited. That's an example of fixed mindset thinking. That can cause you to neglect other areas you could be interested in—and could become good at. And if you are overly narrow or are committed to one area, could that prevent you from developing interests and expertise that you need to succeed?

As the world becomes more interconnected, people who can "bridge" connections between art, technology, and the social sciences become more valuable. Many advances in business and science occur when people with different backgrounds, from different fields, come together. People see new connections between fields that maybe hadn't been seen before. For example, Billy Bean, head of baseball operations for Major League Baseball team Oakland A's, used analytics in new and innovative ways for his baseball team. This also explains the rise in the prominence of liberal arts grads in technology companies. They are the people who can see the big picture, and who can connect the dots and tell the story.

Finding your passion or developing your passion? The latter is far more exciting!

What could you get passionate about?
Hints: Leverage your strengths and superpowers. What are you good at?

Consider these potential interests (not an exhaustive list): hobbies, art, uplifting others, music, learning, simplifying, creating, investing, health and fitness, animals, career, taking action, faith, travel, people, politics, causes, nature, food, and wine.

Think about combining your strengths with a possible new interest. What can you "bridge"? For example, if you love connecting with others, then introducing people who have common interests, such as food and wine, can be special and fun. What could you create?

What new things would you like to try?

What one new thing will you try this month?
Hint: Check out the article, "A Look at the Incredible Benefits of Trying New Things," by Larry Alton for ideas (HuffPost, May 15, 2017).

List new possible passions you might develop:
1.
2.
3.

Now you've found your passions – or have you? How could you put even more passion behind your purpose and into your work?

Step 3: Make a Commitment - Allow Your Passion to Follow

Here's the secret I've learned to developing more passion at work and in life. It's to commit to something.

"Do what you love and never work." Confucius

I think there is a lot of truth to Confucius's proclamation about work. Decide to fall in love with something about your work and let passion follow. That way, you'll never "work" again.

Bo Eason has been one of my coaches. A former NFL safety for the Houston Oilers, an actor, and a playwright, Bo is now an in-demand speaker and author dedicated to helping others tap the power of their personal story to become effective, persuasive communicators.

Here's Bo on passion and commitment: "Since I talk a lot about dreams and becoming the best, you ask me a lot about how to find what you're passionate about. Fair question. But you know what? I never go down that road. I just don't."

"I don't know who made up, 'You've got to do what you love,' or 'You've got to follow your passion.' I've never really done that. I commit somewhere and then I find my passion. People will say, 'Bo, you've got to follow your passion. You've got to do what you love.' And I say, 'No. You've got to commit and then you'll find out what you love and what you're passionate about. I don't follow my passion. My passion follows me.'"

"Whether that was playing in the NFL or writing a play and performing it in New York City or being a speaker, I'm not following my passion in those areas. My passion is following me. I commit to those areas and the hard work it takes, and then my passion follows me."

"The problem is that most people think they're going to make a mistake. They think they're going to choose wrongly and waste ten or twenty years committing to something.

You're not going to waste those years.

You're going to learn the principles of what it takes to be the best. You're going to learn the principles of commitment. You're going to measure yourself and see what you're made of. That translates to any occupation, that translates to a good marriage, and it translates to great parenting.

All you've got to do is commit. If it's the wrong thing, that will reveal itself to you."[39]

Bo's views on commitment resonate with mine.

"Passion is not something you follow. It's something that will follow you as you put in the hard work to become valuable to the world."

Cal Newport

Here's what I've personally experienced. Developing rare and valuable skills will lead to you to far greater career satisfaction. They help you stand out as an expert. That gives you more options and control over your career. You develop passion for a field you have profound expertise in.

Writing this chapter has caused me to reflect on what I've been most passionate about in my career and life. Growing up, it was baseball and skiing. Lifelong learning has always been a passion. Cycling is still a passion and years ago, I went on a solo 1100-mile ride from Chicago to Jacksonville, Florida. Developing talent acquisition and development expertise early in my corporate career was a passion.

Then becoming a leader and operating as the top human resources executive in a fast growing, publicly traded company in the medical device industry was a passion. Starting a new career twenty years ago, becoming an executive coach and author who shows C-suite level leaders how to reinvent and create massive value is a great passion. Growing in my faith with a committed group of eleven Christian men I meet every Saturday morning is my passion. Being the best husband, father, and grandfather I can be – and leading my family, our Fabulous Fourteen – is my greatest passion.

I've been deeply committed to each of these passions. Some of these things I didn't know much about when I started. Some of these passions I'm still a novice in, and I am still very much on a journey.

But with commitment, I'm getting better and – in a few cases – knocking on the door of mastery. Some things were once passions but are no longer passions. Other things have become passions over the years. Many will be passions for as long as I'm on this earth. Make the commitment and the passion will follow.

That's what Andy Mackie did.

The Harmonica Man

He should have been dead.

In his early-sixties, after nine heart surgeries and taking fifteen different medications, the Scottish-born retired horse trainer was barely hanging on. Sick and tired of being sick and tired, and unsure how many days left he had on this earth, he desired to finish his life with meaning and purpose.

Life hadn't been easy. He lived by himself in a camper. His greatest passion was to play folk music and teach others music. He had a difficult time breathing and the side effects of his medications made him miserable. So Andy Mackie made two decisions. First, he decided to quit taking all medication. Second, he would try to give as many people the gift of music as he physically could.

He called the local school in Jefferson County, Washington, and asked if he could teach the students harmonica. A willing teacher agreed. He started with kindergartners – five and six years old. His sponsoring teacher said it was a good learning experience for all. It was fun for the kids and the teacher learned to play, too. Word spread and pretty soon Andy was teaching kids of all grades, and other schools wanted him, too. The teachers said the kids so looked forward to Andy's visits that it improved performance and behavior in the classroom. The kids said, "He taught us a lot."

Andy saved the money he would have spent on medications to buy and give away 300 harmonicas with lessons. When he didn't die the next month, he bought a few hundred more. He went from school to school. Before you knew it, it was 13 years and 20,000 harmonicas later.

To keep the kids interested in music as they got older, he spent the bulk of his social security monthly payment making three-string "strum sticks." He's given out thousands of these strum sticks. He has purchased instruments in stores for kids with special interests and provided free lessons for everyone by getting the older kids to teach the younger ones. He's taught not only harmonica and strum sticks, but fiddle, mandolin, and guitar to students.

The result is truly unique. Andy said, "Music is a gift. You give it away and you get to keep it forever."

Everywhere you go and everyone you meet, everyone in Jefferson County has the same genuine passion for fiddle music. Largely due to one man: Andy Mackie.

Andy has words of wisdom for children, "Do your best. Even if you don't succeed at harmonica, the fact that you've given your best will open doors for you to find something that you'll be good at. You'll find that. And that's a good life lesson."

Andy believes his decision to teach music is what gave his life purpose and passion and kept him alive 13 years after he had been so ill. He said, "Having touched the lives of all these kids, Bill Gates doesn't feel any richer inside than I do."

When Andy received a $5,000 donation from an appreciative parent, he hired a teacher who showed the kids how to make the strum sticks. This gift was the catalyst for the Andy Mackie Music Foundation.[40]

Eight years after Andy's passing, they continue on with Andy's passion of giving children the lifelong gift of music. That's quite an impact!

Andy Mackie's purpose*: To enrich the lives of children through the gift of music.*

Take inventory your passions. Try new things to develop new ones. Commit and let the passion follow. These are techniques to ignite greater passion in your life. What will be your passion plan to inject that jet fuel of passion into your purpose and make that great impact you were born to make?

What will you commit to?

Chapter 5: Turbocharge Your Productivity

Recraft Your Role

There's a big problem with work. Most people feel unsatisfied. Stuck in the daily grind. Going through the motions. They're not very purposeful or passionate about their work. Or maybe even in their lives. How about you?

In an ideal world, your work life would be intrinsically motivating and full of purpose. But too often, it isn't. If you feel this way, you aren't alone. What do you do if you're stuck in a job or career that you once enjoyed, but now you find your heart is no longer in it?

According to a Gallup Workplace article from October of 2019, just 7% of people in the US workplace describe themselves as "fully optimized."[41]

Optimized workers feel a sense of purpose and well-being. They possess the ability to use their purposes, values, and passions to create impact.

There is some encouraging news that our job could be more fulfilling: *The 2019 Workforce Purpose Index* survey conducted by Imperative reported that "74% believe more fulfillment (think impact) is possible in their current job."[42]

Consider these two questions:

Do you find the work you are doing each day is purposeful?

Are you able to create the impact you would like from your work each day?

If the answer is a "no" or "only somewhat purposeful or impactful," what do you do?

You have three choices. The first choice is to be dissatisfied and unfulfilled in your job. The second choice is to seek another job in the hope your new job will be a better fit for you. The third choice is to change your current perspective and approach about work and intentionally bring more purpose, passion, and impact into your current role.

This problem applies to those making $30,000 per year to those making $300,000 to $3,000,000 a year. Loving your job is not predicted by income or education levels. And there's no income level at which people are not desperately searching for purpose and desiring to create an impact.

The good news: There are always approaches to reimagine, re-envision, reinvent your uninspired professional existence, and reshape your role that is better aligned to your gifts, values, purpose, and passions. You consciously design your role to create more joy for you and value for your stakeholders. This task is called recrafting your role.

Back to work that lacks purpose and/or impact. Your first choice, disliking but staying at your job, is unspeakably painful. Unfortunately, it's the option where too many people default to. Disliking your job and staying there is a bad choice and perpetuates your misery. Maybe, at some point, you'll quit for an opportunity where you hope the grass is greener, and then you'll likely find that it is not. Then you find another job, face the same problem, and wonder why you can't find joy in your work.

If you don't dig deeper to understand and apply your unique gifts, purpose, and passions, and discover how to recraft your role in a way that reflects the real you, you will come to the realization that you took your problem with you. The real problem is you and your approach to work.

The second choice is leaving your job to find a new one. The past few years, with a roaring economy and a red-hot job market, perhaps too many people have chosen to quit their jobs, since they have no shortage of external opportunities, rather than first recrafting their jobs. Quitting prematurely can result in regret down the road, leaving you to wonder, "Did I do everything I could to succeed in that job? Did I leave too early? Even though I was dissatisfied, were there other ways to approach my role and work I could have explored?"

There are times when it is necessary to quit and move on. At the end of this chapter I'll share ideas for when to know it's time to cash in your chips and repot yourself in another place.

The focus on this chapter will be choice number three, recrafting your role. I'll show you step-by-step how to recraft your role so you can gain more purpose and passion from work while you create more value too.

In today's knowledge and service economy, most people have wide latitude to do what they do and how they do it. You have a high level of personal discretion as to how you go about your work. That allows you to recraft your role, to bring in the ingredients that are unique to you, into your work, where you spend the majority of your waking hours.

"Work gives you meaning and purpose and life is empty without it."
Stephen Hawking

In addition to bringing more purpose, passion and creating more impact with your work, if you need any more motivation to recraft your job, there's a villain looming that would like nothing more than to take your job. There are actions you can take to mitigate the threat of that villain, so make sure you control what you can in order to futureproof yourself.

The Threat of Artificial Intelligence

Here's a frightening threat that you face if you work for a living. We read and hear about the threat in the media. More and more jobs are being eliminated due to outsourcing and/or artificial intelligence.

As you likely know, the combination of globalization and technology allow for many jobs to be performed anywhere in the world. It's not just outsourcing in manufacturing. These trends have hit the white-collar category full throttle. For example, legal and accounting work is increasingly being outsourced to India and the Philippines. Platforms like Upwork and Fiverr allow easy access to professionals in virtually any occupation to be hired for a gig, rather inexpensively, who deliver high-quality work products at a fraction of the cost in the US and in other western industrialized countries.

If outsourcing isn't a big enough threat, the rise of Artificial Intelligence will prove to be a job killer today and in the next two decades to come. Former Treasury Secretary Larry Summers says technology and its disruptive force will be "the defining economic feature of our era."

Oxford researchers Carl Benedikt Frey and Michael Osborne estimate that forty-seven percent of American jobs are at a high risk of automation by the mid-2030s. The McKinsey Global Institute estimates that forty-two percent of workers could be displaced by 2030. While the adoption of AI and technology will create certain STEM-type (Science, Technology, Engineering and Mathematics-based) jobs, it will displace far more jobs that it will create.[43]

The Antidote to AI – Bring Your Humanity to Work!

While the growth of AI will undoubtedly create technical jobs, there's no doubt it will overall be a job killer and obliterate many jobs as we know them today. So how do you survive and thrive in a world increasingly affected by AI? How do you make yourself more marketable – even if outsourcing or AI has impacted you? You master and apply your uniquely human skills.

Consider the comments of Jack Ma, founder and CEO of Alibaba, China's largest company, which uses AI extensively. At the World Economic Forum, Ma implored the audience that we need to educate our children and today's workers to master skills that machines cannot.

Ma commented, "Everything we teach should be different from machines. Only by changing education can our children compete with machines. Robots could replace as many as eight hundred million jobs by 2030. Education is a big challenge now. If we do not change the way we teach, thirty years from now we will be in trouble. The way we teach the things we teach our kids, things from the past two hundred years, is knowledge based, and we cannot teach our kids to compete with machines. They are smarter. Teachers must stop teaching knowledge – machines are smarter. We must teach something unique, so that a machine can never catch up with us. These are the soft skills we must teach our children. Values, believing, independent thinking, teamwork, and care for others. These are the soft parts. Knowledge will not teach you that. That's why we should teach our kids sports, music, painting, art – to make sure humans are different. Everything we teach should be different from machines. If the machine can do it better, you have to think about it."[44]

Andrew McAfee, MIT researcher and author of the book, *Machine Platform Crowd: Harnessing Our Digital Future,* writes that the most common question he receives is:

"Which abilities will continue to be uniquely human as technology races ahead?"

He writes "Digital technologies do a poor job of satisfying most of our social drives. So, work that taps into these drives will likely continue to be done by people for some time to come. Such work includes tasks that require empathy, leadership, teamwork and coaching."[45]

These high-social skills will become even more valuable than the advanced quantitative ones. Let's make sure we're focusing on developing and demonstrating these in our roles. We must recraft our roles to incorporate these important skills.

Firms like Towers Watson and Oxford Economics report the skills employers will need most in the next five to ten years are not the left-brain thinking skills like business acumen, analysis, or P&L management. Rather, employers seek individuals who are excellent communicators, relationships builders, collaborators, brainstormers, and empathizers. The ability to work with diverse team members, show cultural sensitivity, and create an environment that is purposeful and focused is paramount. These are the right brain skills of personal and social interactions.

Geoff Colvin, author of *Humans are Underrated: What High Achievers Know That Machines Never Will,* writes, "The new high-value skills are part of our deepest nature, the abilities that literally define us as humans: sensing the thoughts and feelings of others, working productively in groups, building relationships, solving problems together, expressing ourselves with greater power than logic can ever achieve. These are fundamentally different types of skills than those the economy has valued most highly in the past.

As a result, the meaning of great performance has changed. "It used to be that you had to be good at being machine-like. Now, increasingly you have to be good at being a person. Great performance requires us to be intensely human beings."[46]

STEM jobs are important, but important isn't the same as high-value or well-paid. In the future, engineers will stay in demand, but the most valuable engineers will not be geniuses in cubicles; rather, they'll be those who can build relationships, brainstorm, collaborate, and lead.

For centuries people have improved their living standards by mastering new skills that a new economy rewards. The skills that are becoming most valuable now, the skills of deeply human interaction, are not like other skills.

The ability of employees to engage customers with humor, energy and generosity is crucial to creating value in an experience that is not, on its face, all that appealing."

The concept of Emotional Intelligence, popularized by former New York Times brain science journalist and author Daniel Goleman, found that employees who perform at the highest levels demonstrate self-awareness, self-management, social awareness, and relationship capabilities. These specific skills include optimism, empathy, transparency, adaptability, influence, collaboration, leadership, and conflict management.[47]

In *Late Bloomers: The Power of Patience in a World Obsessed with Early Achievement,* author Rich Karlgaard writes that people 30 and over have six unique strengths that give them a leg up in a world obsessed with youth, in a world that is increasingly being changed by artificial intelligence and technological advances. He identifies these "late bloomer strengths" as:

1. Curiosity
Curiosity has long-term health benefits, playing "an important role in maintaining cognitive function, mental health, and physical health in older adults."

2. Compassion
Goes beyond empathy to generate action to help the other person.

3. Resilience
Allows for those knocked down by life to come back stronger than ever. Reframing adversity into the life stories we tell

91

ourselves is a key strategy that people tend to learn over time.

4. Equanimity

A mental calmness, composure and evenness of temper.

5. Insight

Insights are the result of us drawing on our full mental library of experience, patterns, and context, yielding an idea of extraordinary value. Our yield of useful insights improves as we age, giving a distinct advantage to late bloomers.

6. Wisdom

How does wisdom manifest itself in late bloomers? Wisdom increases rather than declines with age and experience. Though our pure cognitive speed may deteriorate, what doesn't decrease is reasoning and cognition that is based on knowledge and experience.

Karlgaard concludes, "Why does wisdom grow with age? Aging is associated with a shift in brain activity. Myelin continues to increase well into middle age. It's white matter that acts like insulation on a wire, making neurological connections work more efficiently. Gives 'greater bandwidth.' Wisdom isn't bequeathed. It's earned. And all these qualities – curiosity, compassion, resilience, equanimity, insight and wisdom – are conferred only with time."[48]

High-Value Skills for the Present and Future

It's clear the skills that are seen as high-value ones are the ones that make us uniquely human.

Are you using your uniquely human, high-value skills to create value for you and your stakeholders?

As you master these skills, you become increasingly valuable to your employer and clients. If you lose your job, your mastery of these skills will allow you to stay ahead of your competition and find another role more quickly.

The most frequently cited non-technical skills companies and organizations seek are:

Empathy, Leadership, Teamwork, Coaching, Communication, Relationship Building, Collaboration, Brainstorming, Cultural Sensitivity, Problem-solving Skills, Storytelling, Generosity, and Energy.

It stands to reason if you seek to get more juice from your work, create more value for your stakeholders and futureproof yourself, you are going to purposefully and intentionally build and deploy these high-value skills.

You've Already Got What It Takes

Only other humans can satisfy our deepest interpersonal needs. Our hardwiring from tens of thousands of years make us social beings, needing personal relationships in order to survive. We want and need to work with other people to solve problems, to tell and listen to stories, and to create new ideas. If we didn't do these things 20,000 years ago, we perished. The evidence is clear that groups that have thrived are those whose members possess the most essentially, deeply human abilities – empathy, social awareness, storytelling, collaborating, problem-solving, and relationship building. Since you've already got what it takes, what about recrafting your role to become more human?

The questions for you to reflect on and answer in your logbook are:

How do you assess your proficiency in each of the high-value skills, on a scale of 1 to 10, with one being very low and ten being very high?

How frequently do you use each of these skills in your role, on a scale of 1 to 10, with one being not at all and ten being frequently?

Is there an opportunity to use each of these skills in your role, on a scale of 1 to 10, with one being not at all and ten being frequently?

What would be the benefit if you could use more of these high value skills in your role?

Know the Two Categories of Work

Thinking about your job, write down the deliverables you are responsible for producing. These work deliverables are also called "jobs to be done." You get paid to deliver results. What are those? Write them down.

Done? Good. Now in your logbook, draw a line vertically down the center of the page. On the left side, write "Algorithmic." On the right side, write "Heuristic." What do these words mean?

As Daniel Pink shows us in his book, *Drive: The Surprising Truth About What Motivates Us,* what we do on the job or what we learn in school is divided into two categories.

The first category of work is *algorithmic*, which means you follow a set of instructions to get to a conclusion or outcome. Most work in the twentieth century was algorithmic. Examples would be fast-food preparation, grocery checkout, or production assembly. Increasingly, algorithmic work is being done using automation or it is being outsourced to locations where it can be conducted more cheaply. White-collar jobs in accounting, law, and computer programming that are made up of mostly following routines are not immune either. If you must follow a set of rules or a formula to deliver your work product, that work is algorithmic. Algorithmic work is vulnerable to disruption and puts you at risk.

The second category of work is called *heuristic*, meaning work where you must experiment with different variables and possibilities and then create a novel solution. Writing a book, creating an advertising campaign, operating as a community organizer, helping a patient deal with her suffering, and encouraging patients or clients are examples of work that is mostly heuristic. Work of this sort requires artistic, creative, persuasive, and empathetic skills. This type of work cannot be outsourced easily or done using artificial intelligence.

Reflecting on the deliverables you have just listed in your logbook, put them in the category that fits best. Algorithmic or heuristic. Is there a little bit in both categories? Every work activity is more one than the other. If it is mostly algorithmic, then put it on the left side of your paper.

What do the results of this exercise tell you? If most of your deliverables are algorithmic, you are vulnerable. To futureproof yourself, you need to make your work more heuristic, or prepare to find another job.

The more heuristic you can make your work, the more valuable you are to your employer, clients, and other stakeholders. One of the ways you make your work heuristic is by bringing those high-value human skills to bear that we identified. Empathy, coaching, listening, storytelling, leading, collaborating, and generosity are good ones to deploy.

By committing to develop these high-value skills, and continuing to reinvent yourself, you make yourself more valuable. That opens up more options to you to create the impact you are capable of making through your work. This works for every job - including fast-food restaurant workers like Art Mason.

Making People Smile

At age 59, Art Mason, a friendly and sociable man, had been retired for three months from his factory job. Art had never married. He lived alone and was bored.

One day while dining at his local McDonald's restaurant, Art had a discussion with the manager. The manager asked Art to work there for a few weeks to cover staff vacations. Art agreed to give it a try.

Twenty-nine years later, at the tender age of 88, Art is still at your service. He says he retired once and it didn't work too well for him.

Art Mason loves making people smile. And he's a favorite at the McDonald's in Wayzata, Minnesota. He sits behind the drive-thru window. His customers drive out of their way to place an order when they know Art is working.

It can be hard to find sunshine during a Minnesota winter, but Art provides plenty.

Someone saw a McDonald's pin on his hat and then decided to bring him another pin for his hat. Then another customer gave him a pin, and another. A tradition was born. To date, Art's customers have given him more than 1,000 pins! Art Mason serves happy meals.

"I love Art! Art's awesome. Yay, Art!" Amy Little says as she approaches Art Mason's drive-thru window.

"Good morning!" Art shares a broad smile as he slides open the drive-thru pay window to greet Amy. The two laugh – first Art and then Amy. The sequence is not uncommon. Art's laughter is contagious.

"He is just the sweetest, sweetest guy," Melissa Wildermuth says. "So happy, so happy, like every day's a great new day for him."

"How 'bout two small Sprites, a Sausage McMuffin and a hash-brown?" Art says as he delivers an order with the enthusiasm of a giddy carnival barker.

"Twenty-nine years! And I'll be 89 in May," Art says.

The temporary worker outlasted the owner, the managers, and every other employee at the restaurant.

"Didn't surprise us a bit," Art's brother, Stan Mason said. "He's got to go. He's got to go."

A social person by nature, Art found the drive-thru to be a perfect fit. It's a daily parade during which he could repeatedly, and literally, reach out and touch someone.

"McDonald's has good food, but I come here every day because of him," customer Patty Kubalak says.

Art's sister-in-law, JoAnne Mason, points to the warm blue scarf around Art's neck. "One of his customers made that for him," she says.

Thousands of people work the drive-thru window at McDonald's and other fast-food restaurants across this country. How many have approached and crafted their roles like Art has? As we know, it's mostly an empty transaction.

Art's smile, warmth, ability to connect, and sense of humor create tremendous goodwill and value for his customers, McDonald's, and himself. He lifts up people and gives them a boost – far more than the caffeine boost of their coffees and Diet Cokes.

Art Mason's purpose is making people smile.

Keep going strong, Art! If only everything else in life could imitate Art.[49]

"The seeds of greatness grow faster in the hearts of those doing work they love than in the bitter hearts of those enslaved by work they despise."
Brendon Burchard, *The Motivation Manifesto*

5 Guiding Principles to Recrafting Your Role

There are five guiding principles to keep in mind as you prepare to recraft your job. They are as follows:

1. Adopt a Sculptor's Mindset
2. Know Your "Jobs to Be Done"
3. Connect Your Job to a Purpose Bigger Than You
4. Own Your Job
5. Become a Massive Value Creator

A more detailed description of each guiding principle follows:

1. Adopt a Sculptor's Mindset

To recraft your job, you need the mindset of a sculptor. A sculptor is a highly creative fine artist who develops ideas for statues or sculptures and makes them come to life in three-dimensional form by joining or molding materials together.

See yourself as a sculptor – like Ra Paulette who we met earlier, the cave sculptor from New Mexico.

Sculptors typically work with materials like stone, marble, glass, metal, wood, or ice. In Ra's case, it's sandstone. They continually seek new ways and materials to make art.

They must exercise a lot of patience to make sure their work comes out the way they imagined it. Sculptors have complete freedom of materials and process. They practice and train and are committed to becoming their best, by learning and applying new skills. Is that what you do?

As you approach your job, how can you sculpt it to bring more of your real self to your work, to create more value, to gain more juice for you, and to add more of your unique touch?

The objective in recrafting your job is for you to not only feel more purpose and passion from your work, but to design your role in a way that creates massive value and impact. In today's world, you've got to create great value for your stakeholders, especially your customers and your company.

Here's a hint: If you have been asking, *"What is this job offering me?"* you've got it backwards.

Start recrafting your job by asking, *"What am I offering this job?"* You'll be surprised what you find when adopting this belief.

Questions for you to reflect on:

What am I offering my job today?

What more could I offer my job today?

2. Know Your "Jobs to Be Done"

Identify the "jobs to be done" that your role fulfills. How do they contribute to meeting the mission and strategies of your organization and customers? What benefits – value – do the jobs provide your co-workers, your customers, your company, and your community? In other words, what is the value of your contributions to all your stakeholders?

Why does your job exist? In most cases, jobs are created because they help another person, make a process more efficient or provide a product or service someone else needs. Jobs exist typically because there's a problem someone else is trying to solve.[50]

The "jobs to be done" concept was introduced by the late Clayton Christensen, professor at Harvard Business School and regarded as one of the world's top experts on innovation and growth. Christensen believed that customers don't really buy products or services; they "hire" them to get a job done. Considering the role you serve in – whether you are self-employed or work for an organization – you have a customer you serve, the one you are accountable to. What are the jobs you do for your customer or client?

As I live in Minnesota, I think about snow removal as an annual job to be done. Each fall, I prepare for this "job to be done." There are several options I can choose to get this job done.

I can hire the snow shoveling out, do it myself, or assign it to a family member – if one is available. Or, possibly, I can just ignore the snow and work my way through and around it – not a very practical option where I live, where we average just under sixty inches of snow each winter. Ignoring the snow and driving and walking on snowpack and ice would be called a "workaround."

Usually, a job to be done begins with the words, *"Help me…,"* or *"Help me avoid…,"* or *"I need to…"* And while products and technologies can come and go, "jobs" persist over time. You still need that snow shoveled or plowed. Individuals and companies that organize themselves around a "job" can differentiate themselves in the market and avoid being disrupted.

There are two dimensions of jobs to be done. The first is the functional, the practical role the product or service meets. Like shoveling the snow.

The second dimension is the emotional or social benefit you get from owning or using the product or service. This might include being the first Tesla owner in your neighborhood. Another example would be the raving fans of Apple products who camp out to be among the first ones to purchase the latest iPhone or new blockbuster product.

You can discover jobs to be done four ways. The first is to observe your current customers and ask them what's most important to them. The second way is to identify the workarounds or compensating behaviors your customers use to get the job done today. This could be creating a tire path in the snowpack for your car to follow, using the snow shoveling example. A third way is to interview and discover why your former customers left. Did they go to a competitor? Did they provide the service or product themselves? Did their needs change? Finally, you can reflect deeply on your own personal experiences to identify the jobs to be done.

If you work for someone else, make sure you know their expectations and deliver on those expectations. What you produce. Your results are the "what" of your performance. If you are new to your job or new with your manager, you'll need to create a track record of delivering on desired results first. You take responsibility for the communication. Discuss with your manager your commitment to producing at a high level. In return for delivering on the "what," you are looking for support for the "how" you go about delivering the results. If you are self-employed, the trustworthiness requirement applies too. Do your clients trust you to deliver? Do you always keep your commitments?

Questions for you to reflect on and answer in your logbook are the following:

What "jobs to be done" do you perform for your clients/customers today?

Would your clients/customers agree those are the jobs they need done today? How about in the future?

What skills and abilities does the job require now? How about in the future?

Are you learning, growing, and reinventing quickly enough so you stay relevant and thrive in the service of your customers?

What if someone took your job? What could they do to create a better experience for your customers?

What are you offering your job? What could you offer your job? Be specific.

How could you make life better for someone through your job?

3. Connect Your Role to a Purpose Bigger Than You

A man came across three masons who were working at chipping chunks of granite from large blocks. The first seemed unhappy at his job, chipping away and frequently looking at his watch. When the man asked what it was that he was doing, the first mason responded, rather curtly, "I'm hammering this stupid rock, and I can't wait 'til 5 p.m. when I can go home."

A second mason, seemingly more interested in his work, was hammering diligently. When asked what it was that he was doing, answered, "Well, I'm molding this block of rock so that it can be used with others to construct a wall. It's not bad work, but I'll sure be glad when it's done."

A third mason was hammering at his block fervently, taking time to stand back and admire his work. He chipped off small pieces until he was satisfied that was the best he could do. When he was questioned about his work he stopped, gazed skyward and proudly proclaimed, "I am building a cathedral!"[51]

Three men, three different attitudes, all doing the same job. The first mason saw his job as only a job. The second mason saw his role as a career. The third mason saw his job as a calling.

You can do the same. You can not only transform your attitude but the quality of your work when you are driven by purpose.

The large, global consulting firm, KPMG, created a purpose for the company. It was to help clients "Inspire Confidence and Empower Change."

To prevent those five words from becoming just a marketing slogan, the top executives sought to connect every leader and manager to the firm's purpose. These executives created and shared their individual purpose statements, and realized they needed to do the same with their teams.

The firm invested in a new kind of training, where the partners learned how to create their purpose statements and share their purpose stories. Then they discovered how to connect their individual purposes and stories to that of the firm's, and to tell the story of the connection to their team members.

This kind of role modeling by leaders was unique in the history of KPMG. It required a level of vulnerability and authenticity never seen before, as the executives shared their own accounts of how they were making a difference.

To encourage their followers to do the same, a *"10,000 Stories Challenge"* was created. Team members were invited to create posters that answered the questions, *"What do you do at KPMG?"* which captured their individual purpose statements and passions and connected them to the firm's purpose.

Participating team members created their purpose statements, such as "I Combat Terrorism" and under the statement added a clarifying sentence, such as "KPMG helps scores of financial institutions prevent money laundering, keeping financial resources out of the hands of terrorists and criminals." Each poster carried the firm's purpose, "Inspire Confidence and Empower Change."

The KPMG *"10,000 Stories Challenge"* was more than met. Twenty-seven thousand people participated. The firm found a brilliant way to connect team members personally with its collective purpose.[52]

Questions for you to reflect on and answer in your logbook are the following:

If you work for an organization, is your purpose congruent with your organization's purpose? If not, how could it be?

If you are a leader, how can you better connect your team members to your organization's purpose?

If you are a leader, how can you show your team members how to create greater value and impact through purpose, passion, and recrafting?

What would be the result if you encouraged, supported and coached team members to create their individual purpose statements, and then invited them to connect to the company's collective purpose?

4. Own Your Job

Your mindset must be that you own your job. You are obsessed with the details and what needs to get done. The what, how, why, who, and when. Be an owner, in every sense of the word – your tasks, your project, and your business. Own the relationships with the stakeholders you manage. Own the value you create. You own it. You are trusted because you are all over the details and everything and everybody to make things happen.

"Those are My Pipes"

Consider the example of Corey Mundle, as reported by Mike Rowe, host of the Discovery Channel show, *Dirty Jobs*. Rowe shares his experience with Mundle at a Hampton Inn. "I left my hotel room this morning to jump out of a perfectly good airplane, and saw part of a man standing in the hallway. His feet were on a ladder. The rest of him was somewhere in the ceiling."

Rowe continued, "I introduced myself, and asked what he was doing. Along with satisfying my natural curiosity, it seemed a good way to delay my appointment with gravity, which I was in no hurry to keep. His name is Corey Mundle. We quickly got to talking."

"Well, Mike, here's the problem," Corey said. "My pipe has a crack in it, and now my hot water is leaking into my laundry room. I've got to turn off my water, replace my old pipe, and get my new one installed before my customers notice there's a problem."

I asked if he needed a hand, and he told me the job wasn't dirty enough. We laughed, and Corey asked if he could have a quick photo. I said sure, assuming he'll return the favor. He asked why I wanted a photo of him, and I said it was because I like his choice of pronouns.

"I like the way you talk about your work," I said. "It's not 'the' hot water, it's 'MY' hot water. It's not 'the' laundry room, it's 'MY' laundry room. It's not 'a' new pipe, it's 'MY' new pipe. Most people don't talk like that about their work. Most people don't own it."

Corey shrugged and said, "This not 'a' job; this is 'MY' job. I'm glad to have it, and I take pride in everything I do."[53]

Corey Mundle is a purpose-driven, passionate contributor who creates great value and impact. He's recrafted his job and made himself irreplaceable.

Questions for you to reflect on and answer in your logbook are as follows:

Do you own your job? What evidence supports your assessment?

Would your stakeholders say you own your job? Why or why not?

5. Become a Massive Value Creator

In today's world, you must create great value. Adopting the mindset of creating more value for your stakeholders – no matter what you do – is key. Take the example of the janitor who saw himself creating far more value than keeping the floor clean.

The year was 1962. When President John F. Kennedy visited the NASA space center, he noticed a janitor mopping the floor. The President left his tour guide and walked over to the man with his hand extended and said, "Hi, I'm Jack Kennedy. What are you doing?"

"Well, Mr. President," the janitor responded, "I'm helping put a man on the moon."[54]

To some people the janitor was only cleaning the building. But his purpose was to help the team make history by sending a man to the moon first and safely bringing him back to earth. He was focused on creating value. No matter how large or small your role, you can contribute to a bigger story by helping your company or organization create value and make an impact.

What's the value you are creating? Is it as impactful as the janitor's purpose at Cape Canaveral?

Many people work in roles and never stop to answer the question, "Does my work produce value?"

How will you add massive value going forward?

How will you futureproof your role and yourself in an increasingly AI and technology-dominated world?

It used to be easy to calculate a person's value in the industrial age. It was a simple productivity formula. The formula was:

Work Productivity = Output of work / Hours of Input

In other words, if you produced two hundred and forty widgets in eight hours, your productivity was thirty widgets per hour. That calculation worked fine for decades, but in today's information age, it fails to calculate value appropriately.

The new formula for measuring value in today's economy is:

Value = Benefits to Stakeholders X Quality X Efficiency

In Morten Hansen's book, *Great at Work: How Top Performers Do Less, Work Better, and Achieve More*, he shares five ways to create more value.[55] They are:

1. Eliminate/reduce activities of little value.
2. Spend more time on activities of high value.
3. Create new activities of high value.
4. Find new ways to improve the quality of your activities.
5. Find ways to do your activities more efficiently.

In looking for ways to create more value, Hansen suggests looking for the "pain points," the intractable problems that plague your customers. There's an old adage, "It's easier to sell aspirin than vitamins." What are the pain points your customers experience that you could help fix? That's a terrific way to create great value.

Another way Hansen recommends adding value is to ask stupid "why" questions. For instance, why do hotels have a reception desk for check-in? Why do we conduct annual performance reviews? Why do we call Monday morning staff meetings? Why do we make presentations filled with slides?

People get trapped into conventional thinking. You only see the current use of a practice, process, or method. You get entrapped and have difficulty solving problems due to a fixation on how work has always been done.

Asking "stupid" questions and crafting some "what ifs" can help you discover a nifty recrafting of your role and lift your satisfaction and performance. Companies get ahead by innovating products and services. The way you get ahead is by innovating your work and creating massive value for others.

Remember, you are not an employee. You are a sculptor of work – an innovator and artist. Hunt for the pain points, ask some stupid questions with a few "what ifs" and you can recraft your role and create value for others. Stick with it and refine it little by little over time.

How will you create greater value from your work?

Lastly, creating value means getting good at the high-value and market-ready skills, and it means committing to excellence. So that means making a commitment to becoming your best. To learning, growing, and reinventing.

What will be your plan to learn, grow, and reinvent?

That may mean taking online courses, listening to those informative podcasts on your way to and from work and at the gym, or getting your data science certificate at night. It may mean reading those books, finding a mentor, hiring a coach, or taking other actions—or combination of actions—that will equip you to create a great impact.

Cal Newport, a professor at Georgetown University and the bestselling author of *So Good They Can't Ignore You,* writes "The best way to recraft your job is to gain and develop rare and valuable skills."

He writes, "Basic economic theory tells us that if you want something that's both rare and valuable, you need something rare and valuable to offer in return—this is Supply and Demand 101. It follows that if you want a great job, you need something of great value to offer in return."[56]

When comedian Steve Martin was interviewed about his memoir, *Born Standing Up,* he discussed his rise in comedy and advice for aspiring performers. His response, "Nobody ever takes my advice, because it's not the answer they wanted to hear. What they want to hear is the mechanics: 'Here's how you get an agent, here's how you write a script,'... But I always say, 'Be so good they can't ignore you.'"[57]

So good, you can't be ignored—like Steve Martin. How can you be so good, they can't ignore you?

Recrafting Your Role: Creating Massive Value through Passion and Commitment

Kristin Machacek Leary is an experienced and successful Chief Human Resources Officer for a global, multi-billion-dollar technology company headquartered in Silicon Valley. Her expertise is accelerating the growth of high-flying companies by partnering with the CEOs, senior leaders, and boards to get the two critical pieces of the puzzle right: culture and people.

With experience in both the technology and medical device worlds, Kristin places an intentional focus in crafting her job in a way that zeroes in on the strategic needs of the business, yet also plays to her strengths and values. She says she never looks at a job description. Instead, she understands the results to be delivered, the jobs-to-be-done, and the relationships that need greatest attention. She then sculpts the job in a way that suits her best. She adds that this approach isn't one she's used only as the leader of her organization. It's the approach she's used since she began her career.

When evaluating an opportunity, Kristin looks for excellent chemistry and values fit with the CEO. Without that fit, Kristin takes a pass. If that step goes well, she undertakes a series of discussions with the CEO to gain a thorough understanding of the purpose of the business and the strategies in place that define success. If she sees promise after this step, she then goes through the same process with her peers-to-be and then tests that alignment from the leadership team with the board of directors in a series of interviews. It's critical to Kristin that everyone is on the same page and that she gains a sense they are "good people with good values."

If their answers to her question don't pass the smell test, Kristin pulls herself out of the running. If she's interested, after careful discernment, she accepts the opportunity, she makes a full and passionate commitment to leading the cultural and people pieces of the business. She says she leans all the way in and goes full out. Kristin says zero percent of her motivation if driven by money. She trusts she'll be rewarded for the value she creates. Her approach is to make a commitment, work hard, and the money will come. So far, that has been a very good strategy.

When you meet Kristin, you find high energy, warmth, and a genuineness that is characteristic of her Minnesota upbringing. A global leader who is out of the country fifty percent of the time, she's equally comfortable meeting with executives anywhere in the world and connecting with operators on the shop floor. She is genuinely interested in people; she asks questions to learn about others and shows empathy and understanding. There is no ego. Everyone is treated the same. Whatever topic you are discussing with her, business, restaurants, mutual friends, places to travel, motorcycles or golf, she's engaged, passionate, and positive. She makes you feel like you are one of her best friends.

People love working with Kristin. And because of her visionary, collaborative, and coaching style and approach, she connects deeply with others. She gets them aligned and motivated to accomplish great things. She amazes her peers with her ability to form deep relationships, create trust, and influence others so quickly after arriving at a new company.

Reflecting on why she approaches her work the way she does, Kristin credits her parents for teaching her to always treat people well and to find and commit to a passion. As a teen, she was one of twenty-eight recognized as a youth leader for the Kiwanis Key Club, representing Minnesota and the Dakotas. It was from that experience she learned about leadership, and she has continued to polish her people skills ever since.

Earlier in her career, Kristin was placed in charge of a global leadership training initiative created by the executive vice president of Human Resources, a man her immediate manager, Dave, reported to. The EVP was impressed with what he had heard about Kristin, but told her that he found her enthusiastic, energetic, and upbeat style phony. He suggested to her that she quit being so happy and positive and take a more analytical, serious, and skeptical approach. Given the reporting relationship and power disparity, Kristin listened, but didn't buy it. Fortunately for Kristin, her boss, Dave, had witnessed the discussion. After the EVP left, Dave told her, "He is absolutely wrong. Don't ever lose the passion. Don't listen to him. Continue operating like you do and you'll fly high."

Dave turned out to be right. Kristin didn't change. She continued operating like she had always done. She continued to seek to understand the business situation, to identify the jobs-to-be-done and the ways to create value, and to connect with others to gain their support and help. She sculpted her role so she could lead in a way that fit her best: connecting and inspiring others to greatness, while encouraging them to do the same. That's a technique for creating massive value. [58]

Recraft Like the CEO

From this day forward, I invite you to see yourself as the CEO of your role. Your job is to create massive value and impact. Whatever you do for a living, operate as though you are the CEO, because you are the CEO of your role and your life. You make the decision about how you show up, you make the decision about the experience you create for others, and you make the decision about the degree of excellence by which you serve.

What do CEOs do? They create value. They get results. They are responsible for making their enterprises more valuable by taking great care of their team members, customers, and financial backers. You do the same!

As you think about approaching and tackling your work, ask yourself continually, "What would the CEO do?" If you're the CEO, who is a CEO you admire? Would that CEO, if she were in your role, do what you are doing?

CEOs are ruthless about how they choose to invest their time. They concentrate on the high-value activities that need their attention – those things nobody else in the company can appropriately address, given their unique experience, position, and perspective.

They ask, "Is this activity a good use of my time? Is this activity even necessary? If it is, should I be doing it? Could someone else do it as well or better? If I'm not sure about this activity, will it matter in a couple of months if I'm the one who did it? How about in a year?" Those are excellent questions for you to ask, too.

CEOs work their own agendas first. Otherwise, they can't accomplish their objectives. High-value work comes first; reactive work comes second. You condition others when to expect responses from you. Being the first to respond to emails would mean surrendering your priorities to others. For more on how CEOs operate to create greater impact, see Appendix 1: *Calling All CEOs: A Priority Higher than Profits, Leading with Purpose.*

Recrafting Your Role—The Steps

Recrafting your role is a conscious and intentional process you use to better align your work with your purpose and passion. Recrafting can take you from the verge of quitting your job to redesigning it to one rich in purpose.

"Give me a place to stand and a lever long enough, and I can move the earth."
Archimedes, Greek mathematician

Recrafting is about finding the proverbial lever and using it in a clever way to create greater value.

There are both large and small ways to improve any job. Even incremental improvements can add up to a major increase in job satisfaction. A study from the Mayo Clinic found that physicians who spend about 20 percent of their time doing "work they find most meaningful are at dramatically lower risk for burnout."[59]

While we think of Dr. Martin Luther King Jr. as being a champion of civil rights, he knew a lot about how to recraft a job by giving it his best. He advised, "When you discover what you will be in your life, set out to do it as if God Almighty called you at this particular moment in history to do it. Don't just set out to do a good job. Set out to do such a good job that the living, the dead or the unborn couldn't do it any better."

He continued, "If it falls your lot to be a street sweeper, sweep streets like Michelangelo painted pictures, sweep streets like Beethoven composed music, sweep streets like Leontyne Price sings before the Metropolitan Opera. Sweep streets like Shakespeare wrote poetry. Sweep streets so well that the hosts of heaven and earth will have to pause and say: 'Here lived a great street sweeper who swept his job well.' If you can't be a pine on the top of a hill, be a shrub in the valley. Be the best little shrub on the side of the hill. Be a bush if you can't be a tree. If you can't be a highway, just be a trail. If you can't be a sun, be a star. For it isn't by size that you win or fail. Be the best of whatever you are."[60]

Be the best of whatever you are. That's excellent advice.

Here's how to recraft your role:

1. Open your logbook to a clean sheet of paper. Draw a line down the middle of the page vertically, and draw one across the middle of the page horizontally.

2. You now have four rectangle boxes. Label the four boxes:
    -   Purpose
    -   Tasks
    -   Relationships
    -   Learning

Recraft Your Role

Purpose	Tasks
Relationships	Learning.

3. Read and reflect on the impact work you have completed thus far, the reflections and exercises you've completed in your logbook. You've defined success. You've identified your unique gifts. You are clear about your inviolable values. You've written a purpose statement. You've identified your passions. You know your superpowers. You've done quite a bit of reflective work, and your self-awareness has been heightened.

4. You've read the *Recraft Your Role* section. You've reflected and answered the questions. You know the five guiding principles for recrafting your role. You are prepared to recraft your job.

5. Think about what gives you joy at work. It could be the joy of doing tasks. It might be the energy release when you get to create something new. Perhaps it is interacting with and enjoying people. Maybe it is in learning a new skill and seeing yourself grow. Or maybe it is the excitement at succeeding

on a project. Or it's becoming a master at your craft through hard work and practice. These are the ways to experience passion from your work. Which way resonates most with you? How can you recraft your role to bring more of that joy to work?

6. There are four elements of your work: the purpose you attach to your role; the tasks you perform in executing your role; the relationships with others you enter into in your work together; and the learning, growing, and reinventing you must do to stay relevant and thrive in today's disruptive world.

Purpose

How can you bring more of your purpose to your work like the KPMG team members did? Like the zookeeper who doesn't see cleaning cages and feeding animals as a filthy job, but a moral duty to protect and provide care for the animals. You can find purpose in any job. Why do you do what you do? It's all in how you approach it. Write your ideas down.

Tasks

Tasks are the "what" you do and "how you do it." How could you approach your job tasks in a way that creates more value? Think about the "jobs-to-be-done." The five ways to create more value. How could you perform with more love and excellence? Write your ideas down.

Relationships

Who do you serve? How can you serve others using your purpose as your guide? How can you improve these relationships with co-workers, clients, your boss, and others in your work environment? It can be simple, like taking someone to lunch once a week, or trying to have more meetings in person or on the phone, rather than email. How could you show more empathy and compassion? Write your ideas down.

Learning

What got you here won't get you there. What's made you successful in the past is not guaranteed to make you successful in the future. What new high value skills do you need to develop and apply to stay relevant and to create value? How do you need to reinvent yourself? Write your ideas down.

"The illiterate of the 21st century will not be those who cannot read or write, but those who cannot learn, unlearn and relearn."
Alvin Toffler

Recrafting Wrap Up

As you finish, you've got the makings of your plan to recraft your job and create more value. Make the commitments to what you will do differently, along with the dates you will take your actions. Make sure your commitments and dates are recorded in your logbook.

Recrafting your job is not a "one and done" process. You've now discovered a powerful new tool. You will want to use it continuously and at least quarterly in your quest to work more purposefully, passionately, and productively.

When It's Time to Repot Yourself

Not every job is recraftable to your satisfaction. There are times when you've ridden the proverbial horse as far it will take you. Then it's time to pursue opportunities outside of the organization. How do you know when it's time?

As you reflect on whether the company and your role is the right place for you to work, think of the analogy of a house. A number of years ago, you bought a house that you really liked. Then your family grew. Now, you need a change. What do you do? Do you renovate the house? Do you stay put even though you are a bit cramped? Or do you move? It's a similar decision with your career.

Here's some general guidance:

1. When you join a company, you are hired for a job. While you may be excited about the company and the job, unfortunately, not every manager is a great fit for you. If you find yourself locked into a bad fit with your manager, and you don't see a transfer or other way to get out from under that manager—even after recrafting your role— it's time to leave.

2. Organizations aren't always what they purport to be. If you find the values that are being lived out day-to-day are a bad match for you, despite what may have been stated as the "company values," it's time to go. Continuing there will make you feel like you are compromising your integrity.

3. If you find yourself in a job where you can't bring your purpose to bear in your role—even in a small way—it's time to find a different job.

4. Pick the right pot. Select a company, industry and situation that values what you bring to the party, where your purpose, values, and passions align with the factors that produce success in that organization's environment. When you can leverage what you bring, with what an organization needs, that is a recipe for a great career.

Those four examples are pretty straight forward.

How about if your manager is OK, the values of the company aren't bad, and you can operate in a way that is purposeful? Maybe you still wonder if that's the right place to work. Yes, there are some problems that concern you, but there are good reasons to stay, too. What do you do? Is it time to replant yourself in another pot that will better support your purpose and passions?

"Phil's Advice"

It's hard for me to give you good advice without knowing your situation better, but when I share "Phil's advice," as I have hundreds of times with leaders, perhaps you will find it useful, too.

If you find yourself thinking that a move is what is needed, consider this advice my friend Paul shared with me. Paul is a serial CEO in the technology sector. Several years ago, he was frustrated with his company and was considering leaving the company. He called his mentor, Phil, a partner with a large private equity firm, to express his concerns and seek his advice. Phil's advice was simple.

Phil said, "Identify the two things that are your biggest problems at work that must change in order for you to stay at the company." Paul identified his two biggest issues.

Phil then stated, "Give yourself a reasonable timeframe to fix these concerns." In Paul's case it was six months. Phil then suggested, "Work like heck for the six months to fix the problems. If, at the end of six months, the problems get fixed, you should stay at the company. After all, you fixed the biggest problems."

Phil continued, "If the problems can't be fixed in six months, then you should leave the company. At that point, you will have known you gave it your best shot, yet you were unsuccessful at fixing the problems. You will never look back with regret at your decision to leave. Sometimes in business, problems cannot be fixed. In the words of Kenny Rodgers, it's time to 'fold 'em.'"

That's what Rachel did. She took Phil's advice.

Know When to Fold 'Em

Rachel was a successful leader in her early 50s when she clarified her purpose. While she was defining her purpose, she reflected back on the salient moments of her life, her passions, and her gifts. Here's her story in her words.

"When I was 23 years old, I wanted to see the world and do something physically challenging. Many of my classmates who I had studied abroad with in China traveled to Tibet and raved about it. So a year after graduating from college, and after doing some research, I signed up with an Australian expedition company to do a thirty-day hike in the Himalayas. Traveling on my own, I signed up to join a group of ten other individuals, all strangers to me, ranging in age from twenty-somethings to couples in their thirties and forties. There was one couple in their late forties. I was the only American among this group of Aussies. We had one guide, a bunch of mules who did the heavy lifting, and a handful of sherpas.

"The first few days I was filled with energy and excitement and we trekked an average of thirteen miles each day. As each day went by, my energy and excitement started to wane. The poor sleep, severe altitude sickness, the lack of a warm shower or bath, and eating the same food (mutton, nonetheless) slowly, but surely, chipped away my energy. Little had I appreciated the luxury of standing under a shower with hot water pouring down on me. Little had I appreciated the feeling of being clean, head-to-toe. Little had I appreciated biting into a juicy watermelon or a hot New York-style pizza. Thirty days later, after having summited five mountains ranging from ten to fifteen thousand feet, each time with altitude-induced head-bursting migraines, and only sponge-bathing in a pure, frigid glacial stream, I not only appreciated all of these life luxuries but actually couldn't stop thinking of them. It didn't help that at day twenty, a kerosene tank leaked on the food, resulting in much of the food being discarded. At that point, I learned to appreciate the mutton that I was so tired of as we had to settle with only dahl, rice, and potatoes for the last ten days. By the time we stumbled into the city of Leh, more than three hundred miles away, I was simultaneously thoroughly worn out and fatigued, and deeply proud of my accomplishment, having discovered a deep well of tenacity and potential.

121

"I dug deep into my reserve and courageously faced each day when I had no choice but to tackle the day's trek. I found that I had resilience to keep going. Our group was out in the middle of nowhere, among nature's majestic mountains, lush and fertile landscape, and stark and barren scenery, sometimes not seeing another soul outside of our expedition group for nearly a week. I experienced the forces and beauty of nature and was humbled and awed by its power. I learned that it's when we are pushed to the limits of discomfort, sometimes on the brink of feeling broken, that we have the opportunity to open ourselves up and tap into our reserve to unleash our strength. These lessons from my expedition have stayed with me and carried me into day-to-day life, helping me to navigate through life's twists and turns. It has taught me that power and strength come through vulnerability and openness to move toward the unknown. And this experience confirmed that by embracing discomfort, changes, and new experiences, I am able to surprise myself in discovering the potential that exists within me.

"This experience helped clarify my purpose: *To courageously dig deep to unleash potential as powerful as Nature.* Today I live that purpose in all aspects of my life. I have the confidence to shape my future—and whatever circumstances are thrown my way—when I reflect on my trek in the Himalayas and my purpose.

"The process of clarifying my purpose and identifying my passions caused me to reflect deeply on my career. I've been fortunate to have led companies in the healthcare products sector. About three years ago, I joined a new company to oversee its North American business. After a successful two year run in my first assignment, I was asked to take on even bigger role at the company. On paper, it was an impressive role. I had great responsibility with many people reporting into me, I was compensated well, and served as a valuable member of our company's executive team.

"But I felt something was missing. I wasn't passionate about the company or its culture. The company was very different from the company where I had thrived. It was hierarchical, traditional, and low-energy, run by a CEO who verbally encouraged the opinions of others but his actions didn't support the verbal encouragement. People operated within an environment of fear, and therefore they aspired to "fly under the radar." The climate could be described as collegial at the surface level, but honest, open debate where the best ideas win wasn't truly welcomed or encouraged.

"While there were many positive aspects of the company, I knew this was not the environment or culture for me to thrive long term. I had known this for some time deep inside my soul, but I ignored those feelings, and had grown numb to the situation by throwing myself into my work. My team and I delivered results and put points on the board, while I overlooked the uneasiness of not really fitting in. I was unable to fully commit myself to this company.

"As I embarked on the journey to define my purpose, and reflected on my experience in the Himalayas and how I had lived my life, I strove to operate by courageously digging deep to tap into my potential and live powerfully. That was the true me. And being honest with myself—while I had the big job and the trappings that went along with it—I wasn't living true to my purpose and values. It was at that time that I knew I needed to find a different environment so I could flourish and then help others flourish, too.

"Being clear about my purpose and my passions allowed me to take the courageous next step of resigning. I transitioned with honesty and integrity, leaving the people and position in a good place. This departure gave me an unexpected sense of relief. As I embarked on my search, I felt a sense of great optimism about what the future held. While I was a bit uncertain as I began the journey, and I didn't know my exact destination, I had a strong sense of where I was headed. I believed I would know the destination when I saw it. I was confident I'd find the place where I could dig deep courageously to unleash potential as powerful as nature, and where I could create impact and value for myself and others. I was confident I'd be able to help others be successful and grow in an open and transparent environment. I had great faith the best was yet to come."

Now, six months later, after writing her purpose story, Rachel found her dream job. She accepted the chief executive officer role of a smaller, privately-held company in the women's health industry. She's passionate about the space, the company, and culture, and she is confident she will make a meaningful difference in growing and shaping the future of this company. She states, "Had I not clarified my purpose and my plan to create impact, there is no way I would be in this role today."

As recrafting your role focuses on *how* you'll approach your work, turbocharging your productivity focuses on *what* you will execute in your role. In order to produce more, you'll "do less than obsess" by using the OKR system. Here's how.

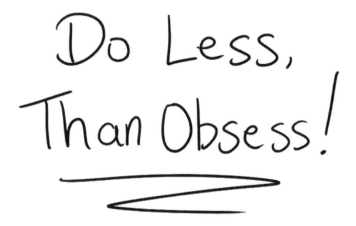

Embrace the Objectives and Key Results (OKR) System to Produce Massively

You've got a game plan to recraft your job. You've identified *how* to bring more of your purpose and uniquely human skills to bear, *how* you'll adjust your tasks to create more value, and *how* you'll leverage relationships to create more value. Recraft your job well and you'll not only bring more juice and passion to your work, but you'll do a better job of serving your customers. You'll create value seen by others, and you make yourself indispensable. You'll stay ahead of your competition and futureproof yourself.

Now, let's focus on turbocharging your productivity. Why?

The #1 purpose for turbocharging your productivity is to give you the time, energy, and resources you need to live the purposeful life of impact you desire.

Now, reflecting on the past month, on a scale of 1 (low) to 10 (high), how productive would you score yourself? What would you like your productivity to be?

Write down your answers in your logbook.

If you are like most folks, there's a gap between your productivity today and where you'd like to be.

Most people, when asked the question, answer that their current productivity level is a 5 or 6. That's usually accompanied by a statement of frustration, because they are working so long and hard. In terms of their desired productivity, it's usually always a 9 or a 10. There's a gap between where they are today and where they need to be.

"So many people are working so hard and achieving so little." Andy Grove

Why wouldn't you want to be more productive? You've got a purpose for your life. You've got your dreams and desires. You can see a path for creating great impact.

But the crazy, busy world gets in your way—distractions, responsibilities at home and work, competing priorities, information overload. You know what it's like. You lose control of your agenda and day, and you lose your focus. You don't produce like you are capable of producing.

The default response, when you aren't as productive as you must be, is to put in more hours or exert more brute force. That's not a sustainable solution. Chances are you already put in long hours. More brute force and hours aren't the answer.

There's a price to be paid when you aren't as productive as you could be. Commitments take more effort, and they cause more stress to see them through. Commitments are sometimes completed in a manner that doesn't represent your best efforts. You miss opportunities, too.

What's the price you pay when you aren't as productive as you could be?

Productivity is a means to an end, not the final destination. Greater productivity is the pathway to a more purposeful, happy and successful life, so that you have the time and energy to experience all life has to offer with those you love. You'll have the time to pursue what matters most to you.

When you're more productive, you get to spend more time and energy on the things that really matter in life: relationships, causes you care deeply about, your faith, travel, hobbies, new experiences, and a myriad of other interests. When you become more productive, you benefit yourself. Yet others benefit, too. Other people get to enjoy more of you. They get you to be present and in the moment with them. That's a great gift! Becoming more productive is the perfect catalyst for getting what you want and living a great life.

What you need is a productivity system that delivers great results. It should be simple, easy to apply, and a pathway to reinventing your productivity. What would it mean to you if you could double or triple your productivity? Or more? That would be a game changer.

"Productivity isn't about being a workhorse, keeping busy or burning the midnight oil. It's more about priorities, planning and fiercely protecting your time." Margarita Tartakovsky

Do you have a productivity system? Can you describe it in ten seconds or less? In my experience, most people stutter and stammer when asked this question. They'll talk about weekly and daily to-do lists and maybe a time management system, such as a Day-Timer or Franklin Covey, or maybe an app they downloaded but don't use consistently.

What's Your Productivity System?

The problem is that time management systems don't drive productivity. Managing your time is important. But let's face it, we all have the same amount of time in a day. Some people get more done, earn more per hour, achieve better results, and are more successful than other people. So, it can't be just about time. To be more productive, you need a system.

I'll guide you through a productivity system that I've used for years and many of my clients use, too. It's called the Objectives and Key Results (OKR) system. The OKR system is about working smarter, not harder. It's particularly popular in fast-paced industries like technology and life sciences where speed and execution are critical. While I didn't know it at the time, the genesis of my productivity system came from a youthful adventure—a long solo bicycle ride I made many years ago.

Running on Empty

When I was twenty-one, I had just graduated from college in four years' time. I found a career job that my major prepared me for. It was a happy time. And, with good fortune, the organization that hired me gave me a start-date two months out at the start of their new quarter. I was ecstatic! I had two more months of loving and celebrating life before starting my career. Life was good![61]

The evening I received and accepted my job offer, a Thursday, I called my brother Steve to tell him the great news of the new job. Steve is twelve years my senior and lives in Frankfort, Kentucky. I was living with my Mom in a southwest suburb of Chicago. Steve congratulated me and said we should celebrate. He asked me to join him at the Jackson Browne concert at Rupp Arena, the home of the University of Kentucky Wildcats, in Lexington. The concert was only eight days away. I happily accepted his offer and told him I'd see him the next week.

With my savings low, and not having better transportation options, I decided to bike it. That's right. Ride my bicycle. Now, I had never biked more than ten miles – ever. And I didn't have a very good bike. I purchased my bike new seven years before when I was a sophomore in high school, for $135, money I had saved from cutting lawns and shoveling snow. It was the bike I rode every day to high school, about two miles from home. This bike was fine to get around town, but taking it on a long trip? We'd soon see. That Panasonic Sport Deluxe was going to get me from Chicago to Kentucky. Hopefully!

I did the math. Steve's house was 360 miles away. If I could manage at least 60 miles a day, in six days I'd be there in time for the concert on Friday night. Having just finished my collegiate baseball career, and in reasonable shape, I thought if the bike stayed together in one piece, I could *probably* complete this journey. But there was no time now for training or even a trial ride. I needed to leave Saturday morning – less than two days away. If all went according to plan, with six days of riding, I'd get to Steve's place – just in time to leave for the concert. And if I couldn't get there, I'd be close enough to call him for a pick-up! My plan was to spend a day or two visiting after the concert, then turn around and pedal back to Chicago.

Looking at the bike loaded with my gear was reminiscent of the bicycle version of the stacked-up truck from the '60s television show, *The Beverly Hillbillies*. I'd be camping along the way, so I installed a rack over the back wheel with three bungee cords used to secure a duffel bag, sleeping bag, and tent. With a little grease on the chain and a shot of air in both tires, I was on my way.

I left very early on Saturday morning, heading east toward Indiana, and - wobbly - rode off into the sunrise. It must have looked like Jethro Bodine of *The Beverly Hillbillies* was riding down the road! Wearing a pair of shorty shorts, tennis shoes with no socks, no shirt, sunglasses and a Chicago White Sox ball cap on backward, I was off for the bike ride of my life.

I set two goals that first day. My "do-able" goal was Fowler, Indiana. After riding east and crossing the Illinois-Indiana state line, I turned right and headed south on Highway 41. That would be a seventy-two-mile ride. My "stretch" goal was West Lafayette, the home of Purdue University, and that was one-hundred miles away. I hit Fowler early in the afternoon and felt strong. Onward to West

Lafayette. I arrived in West Lafayette and didn't want to stop. I surpassed my goal and stretch goal! When I finished my ride the first day, I had landed at a campground in Lebanon, Indiana. One hundred fifty miles – far surpassing my expectations! I found a campsite and enjoyed a dinner of tuna fish in a can and saltine crackers (my staple meal). I drank as much water as I could, and by nightfall, was fast asleep.

The second day, Sunday, I checked my Rand McNally Road Atlas which had state maps of all fifty states and the Canadian provinces. I mapped out a route that would take me around Indianapolis. As I mapped my journey, I couldn't ride on interstates on a bicycle, so my preferred choice was state highways or county roads. I set my "do-able" goal to Franklin, seventy miles away, and a stretch goal to reach Columbus, Indiana, one hundred twenty miles away. I hit Columbus by 5 pm, found a campground and rinsed off and repeated the routine from the previous night. Stretch goal met!

Monday was day three. Frankfort, Kentucky was one-hundred twenty miles away. Today there would be no "do-able" goal – it was Frankfort or bust! Imagine how surprised Steve will be to see me! I thought to myself, "Piece of cake!" And with any luck, I'd get to Steve's house by dinner time and maybe would get to enjoy a piece of cake! The anticipation made me smile and laugh.

The start of the ride went great. After ninety minutes or so, the slope started a nice descent and I made great time without having to pedal too hard. I realized I was in the Ohio River valley and enjoyed the easy cruise downhill and even got to coast a bit. Crossing the river at Madison into Kentucky, I learned that river valleys have two sides. If you go down one side and cross the river, you have to ride up the other side! The Kentucky side of the valley seemed like one continuous incline and the ride was grueling. Uphill in the heat of summer. A grind. But by 5:30 pm that evening, I'd made it to Steve's house.

When I knocked at the door, fresh off one hundred twenty miles in 90+-degree heat, he answered and said, *"What the He**?! And, what are you doing here? I thought you were getting here Friday – and it's Monday – for the concert? Why are you so sweaty? And you stink! How did you get here? And you need to hose off outside before you come in the house!"*

Hanging around his house that week, I totally wore out my welcome with my sister-in-law. It was bliss to relax my tired legs and refuel on everything in their refrigerator.

The concert in Lexington was a blast. Something about hearing Jackson sing his iconic song, *Running on Empty*, hit my heart. Those lyrics were speaking to me.

> Looking out at the road rushing under my wheels
> Looking back at the years gone by like so many summer fields
> In sixty-five I was seventeen and running up one on one
> I don't know where I'm running now, I'm just running on
>
> Running on, running on empty
> Running on, running blind
> Running on, running into the sun
> But I'm running behind
>
> Gotta do what you can just to keep your love alive
> Trying not to confuse it with what you do to survive
> In sixty-nine I was twenty-one and I called the road my own
> I don't know when that road turned, into the road I'm on
>
> Running on, running on empty
> Running on, running blind
> Running on, running into the sun
> But I'm running behind
>
> Everyone I know, everywhere I go
> People need some reason to believe

I don't know about anyone but me
If it takes all night, that'll be all right
If I can get you to smile before I leave

Looking out at the road rushing under my wheels
I don't know how to tell you all just how crazy this life feels
Look around for the friends that I used to turn to pull me through
Looking into their eyes I see them running too

Running on, running on empty
Running on, running blind
Running on, running into the sun
But I'm running behind

Honey you really tempt me
You know the way you look so kind

I'd love to stick around but I'm running behind
You know I don't even know what I'm hoping to find
Running into the sun but I'm running behind

*Credits to Jackson Browne/Swallow Turn Music[62]

And then I had an epiphany!

Instantly, it was apparent this would be the theme for the bike trip – *Running on Empty*! I hung out with Steve for the weekend. I told him my decision. I was taking off on Monday. But I wasn't returning to Chicago. I made a decision to head south. The new destination: Jacksonville, Florida!

My Aunt Vivian had recently moved from a Chicago suburb to Jacksonville. I knew she'd be glad to see me and I could hang out with her for a while in Florida. I plotted the course in my mind and fantasized about the adventure!

Steve thought it was a crazy idea. He tried to talk me out of it, but saw my stubborn streak and knew arguing was hopeless. In a last-ditch attempt to dissuade me, he told some horror stories about hillbillies in southeast Kentucky and asked if I'd seen the movie *Deliverance.* I had seen it and still wasn't scared. Undeterred, he then told me how I'd have to dodge the trucks that hauled coal from the mines, that fly down the backroads, and would run me off the road for sport. Honestly, that story did cause consternation.

He followed with a carrot - a compromise if I agreed to take a bus over the mountains with the bike, he'd spring for the ticket. Without my knowledge, he called our mother, told her what he believed to be my harebrained Florida-ride idea, and asked her to weigh in. She then called me at Steve's house, urging me to return to Chicago, but if I must continue the ride, to please accept Steve's gracious offer. I capitulated. Reluctantly, I agreed to take a "red eye" 12-hour bus ride on Sunday from Frankfort to Elizabeth City, North Carolina, near the Virginia border, which got the bike, my gear, and me over the mountains and on the road in Carolina at 7:00 a.m. on Monday, heading east for the Atlantic coast.

Despite a fitful night's sleep on the bus, I made it to New Bern, one hundred twenty-five miles from Elizabeth City. The next day's ride took me ninety miles to Wilmington. The following day's ride was short at seventy-five miles and I found myself in the vacation town of Myrtle Beach, South Carolina. Sometime during the Carolina ride, I offered myself a challenge. If I reached Myrtle Beach in three days, I'd give myself a little reward of a few nights in a hotel to enjoy this fun beach town. I made it and found a cheap hotel between a couple of honkytonks and across the street from the beach.

While in the beach town, I did what most red-blooded 21-year old young men would do in the summer at Myrtle Beach. I can't say my training habits were the best, but I have fun memories of fun in the sun, cute tan girls, and hanging out at the beachside bars at night.

Charleston was next in my sights. My goal was to find an affordable hotel in Charleston, which at one hundred ten miles, would be a challenging stretch goal. Riding to Charleston from Myrtle Beach was tough. It was hot and humid, and not to mention, I rode against a ridiculously strong headwind. It engulfed me with the smell of roadkill ahead for what seemed like the entire ride. It was one-hundred-and-ten painful miles. A brutal, all-day grind.

At 6 p.m., as I entered Charleston, I was greeted with the sight of the John P. Grace Memorial Bridge, a nearly three-mile-long cantilever bridge that had two ascents and two descents. It had a peak clearance of one-hundred fifty-five feet to the Copper River below. The open grate bottom allowed me to see the water straight down. It looked like it was far more than one hundred fifty feet below the bridge – it looked like an easy one thousand feet! There were no bike lanes, only a narrow sidewalk, barely wide enough for me to ride. To my left was the rush hour traffic, zooming by, only an arm's length away. To my right was an open rail contraption that served as the "guard rail" that kept me from falling into the river. I think an angel was riding for me! I was never so happy to safely complete a ride over a bridge.

Finally, I welcomed what would soon be the conclusion of the ride. When I found a cheap motel with its "Vacancy" sign on in Charleston, I was sweaty, exhausted, and yet grateful to have found a place to hole up for the night. The front desk clerk took one look at me and said there were no vacancies. I still get a chuckle at the look on his face. My appearance must have scared him!

A mile down the road, there was another cheap motel. The front desk manager took mercy on me and I got my room. A bed never felt so good. I was so grateful for shelter!

Savannah was only one hundred miles the next day and the ride went well. Then on to Brunswick, Georgia, for what was an easy, albeit hot, eighty-five-mile ride. Finally, Brunswick to Jacksonville was the next day's ride and the journey was complete.

Aunt Vivian was sure surprised to find me on her doorstep. She was gracious and took me in, as I expected. She fed me, let me sleep and get my mojo back after my long journey. What an experience! Eleven-hundred miles in ten days of riding. I rode every foot of the journey by myself. So many memories and life lessons.

Overview of the Objective and Key Result (OKR) System

Reflecting on my youthful adventure and successful bike journey, what became clear was that I stumbled upon a productivity system that enabled me to produce and perform at a high level.

First, I had an *objective.* That objective was initially to arrive safely in Kentucky in six days or less. Once that objective was completed in three days, the new objective was to arrive safely in Jacksonville in ten days or less.

An objective is simply the *what* that is to be achieved, no more and no less. My objective was to safely reach my destination within a designated time frame.

Secondly, I created *key results* for my ride. Key results are the *how* of accomplishing the objective. Key results should be specific, measurable, and verifiable.

I had three key results for my ride to Florida. They were to average eighty miles or more each day, maintain the bike daily, and stay healthy, safe, and positive each day. Each key result was supported by three to five *big rocks*, as I call them. Think of the *big rocks* as the daily actions necessary to achieve the key results. Over time, the big rocks add up. Before you know it, you've achieved the result. Key results accomplished roll up to an objective being achieved.

Here are my OKRs for the bike ride from Kentucky to Florida.

Objective:
Arrive safely in Jacksonville in 10 days or less.

Key Results:
1. Average eighty miles or more each day.
- Choose a "do-able" ride of 80 miles and a "stretch" ride of 100+ miles each day.
- Average 16 to 18 miles per hour.
- Hit the road by 7 a.m.

2. Maintain the bike to ensure operability 98% of dedicated daily ride time.
- Grease the chain and derailleur.
- Check tire pressure and condition.
- Tighten loose parts and clean and repair as necessary.
- Clean off road gunk and dirt.

3. Stay healthy, safe, and optimistic each day.
- Hydrate the night before for next day's ride by drinking a gallon of water and Gatorade.
- Get nine plus hours of sleep.
- Start the day with a healthy breakfast.
- Stay positive and create fun, challenging contests using M&Ms, ice cream, Mountain Dew as rewards.
- Quit riding for the day if can't average 16 mph.

To accomplish the OKRs, there were three *vital functions* I needed to spend 90% of my time on.
The vital functions that supported my OKRs were:

1. Riding—the act of riding the bike;
2. Fueling—the act of eating and hydrating with water and drinks with electrolytes; and

3. Resting and Recovering—the act of sleeping, taking breaks, meditating, massaging my legs, and planning the next day's ride.

Focusing on the daily key results and big rocks kept me in the present. I didn't worry about tomorrow's ride. I chunked down that daily ride into hourly big rocks. If I'd win my little hourly mileage big rock challenge, I'd treated myself to some M&Ms or maybe a Mountain Dew from a gas station.

If I didn't meet my challenge, no reward. Chunking down the ride gave me a sense of focus and got my competitive juices flowing, creating a tough but do-able challenge. Achieving the hourly challenges and meeting the daily OKRs were tremendously gratifying and motivating. I knew if I accomplished the big rocks, I would definitely meet my "do-able" ride and likely meet my desired stretch ride goal. I'd win the day.

At day's end, I reflected on the ride. What I'd seen, heard, felt, and smelled. The people I met along the way. The terrain and the sights.

As I biked, I reflected on anything that really stood out to me, and I tried to find humor in the mundane ride of eight hours. On one leg of the journey, I saw what appeared to be a snake in my path. But as I approached and got a better view, it was actually a long stick. As someone who was not a fan of snakes, I always had them on my radar. This happened many times. But if I saw what appeared to be only a broken fan belt ahead, and then ignored it, I could see it all of a sudden slither across the road and I'd be startled half to death! I'd simply seen a snake sunning itself on the asphalt. This happened twice!

I reflected on outrunning those dogs that chased me—they made me pedal to the max, but they never caught me! I was proud of my accomplishments. I was strong and fit. You might be surprised at how quickly your legs strengthen, and how those big thigh muscles grow. My confidence grew. I believed that I could do anything I set my mind to. As I won each day, I built momentum.

Before I knew it, I had completed the ride. This bike ride proved to be a transformative experience in my young life. It was quite the journey. What it did that was really important was that it taught me a productivity system that I have used ever since – the OKR system.

Our focus is how you implement the OKR system for you, so you can produce massively.

Yet the OKR productivity system works even better when everyone you work with is on board. When teams, departments, and companies embrace the OKR system, it can be the "X Factor." Companies that embrace an OKR system across their organization get a tremendous level of clarity, focus, and alignment. CEOs and other senior leaders at organizations should consider an OKR system because the lack of alignment and focus are major obstacles for most companies. Studies have shown that only 7% fully understand their company's strategies and key initiatives.

> *"Unchecked complexity is the silent killer of growth."*
> James Allen, Bain & Company

Andy Grove, the late former CEO of Intel, has been credited as the creator of the OKR system. John Doerr, who was a young engineer at Intel when Grove implemented the system, has introduced it to many Silicon Valley-based firms in his role at the venture capital firm Kleiner Perkins. Doerr's book, *Measure What Matters: How Google, Bono and the Gates Foundation Rock the World with OKRs*, profiles a number of companies and non-profits, including the ONE campaign, and their experience using the OKRs.

Here's how the ONE campaign, founded by Bono, used the OKR system to hang their passion on.

"Provide a Frame to Hang Our Passion On"

When you think of Bono, you might think of his charisma as the front man and vocalist for the band U2. Or you might think of his activism for social justice causes, particularly in Africa. But you probably wouldn't think Bono as an advocate for OKRs.

His first initiative in Africa, the Jubilee 2000 Global Initiative, led to $100 billion in debt relief for the world's poorest countries. Then, equipped with a startup grant from the Gates Foundation, Bono co-founded DATA (Debt, AIDS, Trade, Africa), a global advocacy organization for public policy change.

In 2004, Bono launched the ONE campaign to catalyze a nonpartisan, grassroots, and activist coalition. It's the outside-facing complement to DATA's inside game. Like many well-meaning non-profits, a danger for them is "boiling the ocean." In other words, with so many needs, there is no prioritization. In trying to do too much, there is too little focus. And this brings sub-optimal results, frustration, and limited impact.

To prevent the "boiling the ocean" syndrome and to provide maximum clarity, ONE needed to embrace a concept called "factivism," or fact-based activism. According to David Lane, CEO, "We needed a process of discipline to keep us from trying to do everything." You can only go so far without process. Enter the OKR process.

Bono elaborated, "We went after universal access to anti-AIDS drugs, another clear goal. And I must say, people did laugh in our face: 'You are out of your tiny mind. That's impossible. Why fight the most expensive disease?'

"It's because of longitude and latitude. If you live in Malawi, you don't get the pills. If you live in Dublin or Palo Alto, you can get the pills. That doesn't feel right.

140

"In 2019, twenty-one million people are accessing antiretroviral therapies. AIDS-related deaths are down 45% in the last ten years. New HIV infections in children are down by more than half. At this pace, we will see the end of mother-to-child transmission by 2020, to finish the disease off. I believe we will live to see an AIDS-free world in our lifetime."

Bono continued, "OKRs gave us a frame to hang our passion on. And you need that framework because without it your brain is just too abstract. The OKR traffic lights, the color coding – they transformed our board meetings. They sharpened our strategy, our execution, our results. They made us a more effective weapon in the fight against extreme poverty."

"The OKRs have kept us focused on the concrete changes we need to make – hiring staff in Africa, expanding our board, reconnecting with old Jubilee partners, and identifying new networks to turn to for advice."

Objective:
Proactively integrate a broad range of African perspectives into ONE's work, align more closely with African priorities, and share and leverage ONE's political capital to achieve specific policy changes in and toward Africa.

Key Results:
1. Three African-based candidates hired and on-boarded by April, and two African board members approved by July.
2. African Advisory Board in place by July; the board will convene twice by December.
3. Relationships fully developed with a minimum of 10 to 15 leading African thinkers who actively and regularly challenge and guide ONE's policy positions and external work.
4. Undertake four participatory trips to Africa over the course of this year.

Bono stated, "It's not enough to be passionate. So you're passionate – *how* passionate? What actions does your passion lead you to do? Now we can say, "Here is what we've done, and this is the impact it's had.

"If the heart doesn't find a perfect rhythm with the head, then your passion means nothing. And when you have that sort of structure and environment, and the right people, magic is around the corner."

ONE has helped deliver nearly $50 billion in funding for historic health initiatives. That's quite an impact, guided by OKRs.[63]

I've seen my corporate clients get turbocharged results after implementing an OKR system. Since the "how to" of implementing a company-wide OKR system is beyond the scope of this book, let's focus on you – how you can adopt your own OKR system to maximize your personal productivity.

Here and now, you are at an inflection point. You have a choice. You know you can and should be more productive. Are you motivated enough to do something about it? Or do you settle and pay the price for a mediocre performance and missed opportunities? What will you do? Failing to make a choice is itself a choice.

Let's first understand some of challenges that prevent us from being as productive as we could be. Since most people spend 50% or more of their waking hours working, it's imperative that you master the productivity skills that will allow you to gain the biggest return possible on your investment of time and effort.

As you seek to produce more and create more value, beware of the productivity cripplers out there just waiting to derail you. To be productive and perform like you're capable, it's important for you to know and neutralize these productivity cripplers and embrace the productivity catalysts.

Beware of the Productivity Cripplers

To get you started, you should know what gets in the way of high productivity and then make sure you've insulated yourself from their reach. There are four crippling enemies of productivity. They are: 1. Information Overload; 2. Multi-tasking; 3. Distractions; and 4. Reactive, Shallow Work.

Let's break these cripplers down into some more detail.

Information Overload

There is so much information coming at you, so fast, it's impossible to know it all. The global, digital business environment we work in has created this monster. The entire digital universe is expected to reach 44 zettabytes in 2020. That's number 44 with 21 zeros after it! The prospect of staying current and relevant both individually and organizationally begins to feel overwhelming.[64]

Years ago, futurist Buckminster Fuller expressed the idea of the "Knowledge Doubling Curve." He concluded that, until 1900, human knowledge doubled every century. At the end of World War II, knowledge doubled approximately every 25 years. Now, according to IBM, the "internet of things" leads to the doubling of knowledge every 12 hours. There's more information than we can possibly absorb. Instead of being cataloged at a library, it flies at us on every smartphone, tablet, and laptop we own. Our ability to adjust to all this has lagged behind—and it always will. The result is a feeling of being overwhelmed—anxiety and stress.[65]

Multi-tasking

It's a myth that we can multi-task. Yet it has been reported that 28% of our days are spent multi-tasking. Actually, we don't multi-task, we task-switch. CNN reports that when you multi-task, you become dumber. Dumber than being stoned. When you're stoned your IQ goes down only five points. When you multi-task, your IQ goes down ten points!

You can only multi-task when doing an automatic behavior like walking and talking. When you walk with a friend and talk, walking is automatic. You don't give it a thought while talking or listening during your conversation. One is a physical activity and the other is a mental activity. For activities that require your full attention, you can't multi-task. If you try, you task-switch, going back and forth between two areas of concentration. You can't use the same region of the brain simultaneously on a mental task. For example, you can't effectively be on a conference call and read email.

Intense multitasking produces stress. Those who do this are chronic multi-taskers and are less efficient than those who focus on one project at a time. You give yourself acquired ADD. You lose your energy. Don't do it!

Are you still not convinced? Try this. Out loud, count from one to ten as fast as you can. Now, do the same with the first ten letters of the alphabet, A-J.

Now, combine the two: A1-J10, as fast as you can. What happens? It takes longer, you're less accurate, and it's harder. You must slow down and your efficiency drops.

Here's a challenge for you. Commit to not multi-tasking for a week. That means devoting full attention to whatever single thing you're doing. This will reduce stress and make you more productive.

Distractions
When you are focused on deep work, distractions are just waiting to run you aground. Deep work is critical if you want to make an impact on the world. Eric Barker, author of the bestselling book, *Barking Up the Wrong Tree: The Surprising Science Behind Why Everything You Know About Success is (Mostly) Wrong*, writes: "Deep work is so important that we might consider it as the superpower of the 21st century."

Shallow work is comprised of non-cognitively demanding tasks, which you often perform while distracted. These efforts don't create much new value in the world and they are easy to replicate.

You've got to set yourself up for success by eliminating sources of the distractions.

The biggest culprit is not your boss. The biggest culprit sits in your pocket. Your smartphone. According to data collected from Apple, the typical owner pulls out and uses his or her iPhone 96 times per day – over 35,000 times a year. Our smartphones make us dumber.[66]

A recent study showed that people use their smartphones on average five hours a day. And we wonder why we suffer self-imposed "techno-stress." We're busy to the max! You distract yourself, rapidly toggling between tasks. You're mired in multi-tasking, unable to concentrate on one thing. And you feel overwhelmed.

The Wall Street Journal reported that "while our phones offer convenience and diversion, they also breed anxiety." Their extraordinary usefulness gives them an unprecedented hold on our attention and vast influence over our thinking and behavior. As the brain grows dependent on the technology, the research suggests, the intellect weakens.

A study published in the Journal of Experimental Psychology argues, "When people's phones beep or buzz while they're in the middle of a challenging task, their focus wavers and their work gets sloppier—whether they check the phone or not. And when people hear their phone ring but are unable to answer it, their blood pressure spikes, their pulse quickens and their problem-solving skills decline."

In an article in the Journal of the Association for Consumer Research, Dr. Ward and his colleagues wrote that the "integration of smartphones into daily life appears to cause a brain drain that can diminish such vital mental skills as learning, logical reasoning, abstract thought, problem solving and creativity."

All this makes us feel like we must respond 24/7. What we must do is give our minds more room to think. And that means putting some distance between yourself and your phone. So, when doing important work, turn off your phone.

Of course, our phones aren't the only distraction, there are other weapons of mass distraction.

On average, we're disrupted or distracted every three minutes. It takes eleven minutes to regain concentration. Forty percent of the time, you don't return to the task or project you were working on, research states.

Creating a working environment that is as distraction-free as possible is the key to deep work. If you want to make an impact and raise your productivity, curb the distractions.

Doing Reactive Work

You put in the hours. But are you creating value? You can be busy, but so are ants. They are busy being busy. Being busy can feel great. But are you zooming around and accomplishing little or much? If you are like most people, you do what is fun and easy rather than what is hard and necessary.

You pile on work, and then you pile on outside activities. You're addicted to busyness. You're exhausted, yet fearing what you might do without a frenetic schedule. You hurry, unable to be present for even a few moments. This malady has a name: hurry-sickness. You load up stress and anxiety when you are overly busy, and you burn the candle at both ends.

Sadly, it is not just adults. Kids are loaded up with sports and extracurricular activities, classes, and homework assignments. They feel as wiped out as adults.

Most people focus on reactive, shallow work. Shallow work keeps you from getting fired. Deep work gets you promoted.

A McKinsey study found that the average knowledge-worker now spends more than 60% of the workweek engaged in electronic communication and internet searching, with close to 30% of the worker's time dedicated to reading and answering email alone. These kinds of efforts tend not to create much value.

Are You Working
Proactively
or
Reactively?

Do only what creates real value, what's truly important, not what someone else can do. Don't do busy work, either. You know that "busy" and "productive" are two different things. The fun and easy stuff can keep you busy, but you need to devote yourself to what's hard—and necessary. What stretches your capabilities? Shallow work is responding to email, attending meetings, and just moving information around. Deep work is what makes a difference.

This is a war against the productivity cripplers. You'll need to make serious shifts. Make the transition from reacting to creating. Typically, there is very little creation at the office. You choose to work on your agenda, not someone else's. A reply email or text is someone else's agenda.

If you don't use your concentration muscle, it atrophies. It's time to commit to deeper, proactive work. Shift from shallow, reactive work.

You can neutralize the productivity cripplers when you can then embrace the productivity catalysts. When you build these catalysts into your routine, your personal productivity will soar.

Embrace the Productivity Catalysts

There are four catalysts to surge your productivity that are the core of the OKR system. They are: 1. Commit to Your Vital Functions; 2. Select Your OKRs; 3. Choose Your Big Rocks Daily; and 4. Build a Parking Lot.

We'll break down these catalysts into additional detail as follows.

Commit to Your Vital Functions

What are your few vital functions, and how much time do you spend on them? Most people, when introduced to this concept, admit it's a small percentage of their time. You need to drive that percentage higher and higher.

It's imperative you identify and spend the overwhelming percentage of your time on your vital functions. These are the functions of your work that create the greatest value. What are your three vital functions? In my bike ride example, I chose three during that period. They were: Riding, Fueling, and Rest/Recovery. That's how I spent 90% of my time.

By focusing your time and energy on these vital functions, you make the biggest difference. You commit to being world-class at these few things rather than being mediocre at many things. Every role, every endeavor, has functions that make the biggest difference. They are where you bear down to gain huge results. Spend 80 to 90% of your time on your vital functions, doing the work that moves the needle.

Everything doesn't matter equally. Pareto points us in a clear direction with his "20:80" law. The majority of what you want will come from the minority of what you do. Extraordinary results are disproportionately created by fewer actions than most realize. So, let's focus on where you can get extraordinary results by identifying the vital functions that "make it rain" in your role.

In my business as an executive coach to CEOs and senior leaders, I have three vital functions. They are: 1. Coach and Consult; 2. Business Development; and 3. Research and Development.

The three vital functions of my client Bill, who is the global vice president of marketing for an infection control company, are to: 1. Build a team of top talent; 2. Create a high-performance culture; and 3. Align everyone with the new strategy by repositioning the company as a partner to healthcare professionals versus a manufacturer and distributor of products.

The three vital functions of a realtor might be: 1. Prospecting for new clients; 2. Pitching new clients; and 3. Closing contracts.

Now, how can you define your vital functions? If you are self-employed, here's one way. What's your income goal for this year? Divide it by 2,000 hours, to determine your hourly rate. For instance, if your income goal is $250,000, your hourly rate would be $125; $250 would be your hourly rate if you sought to make $500,000; $500 if $1 million was your target; $1000 per hour if $2 million was your goal.

Now ask, "Would I pay someone my hourly rate to do whatever it is I'm doing right now?" If the answer is "No," that's work to delegate – or maybe quit altogether. You can free up time to work your vital functions.

You may be able to type 60 words per minute but your income target is $150 per hour. Should you type that report, that will take three hours, or hire someone for $20 per hour to do it? If you choose to type it, you don't just spend $60 for the project. You cost yourself $450. You can hire free-lance professionals to do all kinds of jobs using Upwork, Fiverr, and Guru.com who will do outstanding work on assignments. Use them while you focus on your high-value creating work. This is a big value creating opportunity. These are your big-value creators!

If you don't own a business or you are paid a base salary, here's another way to determine your vital few.

Rank in order the highest-value work you do. What generates the highest revenue or profitability for your business? What are the highest value jobs-to-be-done? What's the biggest opportunity? Rank these functions to create clarity for yourself. Make a list from one to ten.

You can then take 20% of the 20% of the 20% and continue until you get to the single most important thing! No matter the task, mission, or goal—big or small—start with as large a list as you want, but develop the mindset that you will whittle your way from there to the vital few. Do not stop until you end with the essential top thing. The imperative top thing—just *one* top thing.

Remember, *"You can do anything once you stop trying to do everything."*

Steve Jobs, Apple's late CEO, reduced his vital three functions to one: launching revolutionary new products. He spent up to three hours a day on it. The iPod and retail. Then the iPhone. Then the iPad. What are your vital three? What's your vital one? If Steve Jobs did it, what's your excuse for not doing it?

Joel Osteen is Senior Pastor of Lakewood Church in Houston. He's the CEO of a $100 million enterprise. What's his vital one? Twenty-two minutes on Sunday. That's where he puts 80% of his energy and focus.

Catching a Tiger by the Tail

Cathy is a 40-something, super-energized president of the fastest-growing division of a Fortune 500 company. Operating in more than 100 countries, it's the world's largest consulting services provider to the life sciences and pharmaceutical industries. Cathy was brought on two years ago to integrate a recent acquisition and make it the company's growth engine. Achieving this required hard work and, at times, brute force.

The past year, the division achieved revenue growth of 55%, surpassing expectations. Now, her CEO wants more. Huge opportunities await in China, India, and other growth markets, in addition to the US and Europe. To sustain the growth, Cathy knows she must lead differently and stay highly focused. I introduced her to the idea of vital few functions and she pounced on the concept.

For the upcoming year, Cathy determined the vital functions she must devote her efforts to. They are:

1. Coach her direct reports to reach committed goals.
2. Plan for growth this year and beyond.
3. Inspire others by telling the story of purpose, opportunity, growth, and performance.

Cathy has set a goal of spending 80-90% of her time on them. By saying "No" to unrelated requests and distractions, Cathy believes she will make the best use of her energy and time.

The linchpin function, Cathy acknowledges, is the first. She's empowering her direct reports in a noticeably different way. In the past, when she sensed they were struggling, Cathy tended to backstop them. She knows that has to change. The breadth and growth of her division have made it impossible for her to put her fingerprint on all aspects of the business.

Operating with a CEO mindset, she is determined to rely on her lieutenants to deliver, to continue the growth. As with many fast-growing companies, infrastructure development lagged behind revenue growth. To equip her direct reports to lead, she's worked with her CFO to create P&L's and balanced scorecards to monitor the financial and operational performance of the division.

She's carefully selected her team and given them the tools to manage their respective businesses. She's looking forward to seeing who steps up and really takes the lead. She calls this the Year of Empowerment. She's committed to working with her team to help them create their individual purposes and connect them to the business and show others how to do the same. Cathy is also excited about how she herself will grow as a leader.

Concentrating on the three vital functions will require her to operate at a higher level, giving her the bandwidth to capitalize on acquisition prospects and other opportunities that come her way. Cathy is proactively reinventing herself as a leader and taking her productivity to a whole new level. She's creating massive value.

In summary, the OKR concept is to concentrate on less and accomplish more. Work on what is truly important: your three vital functions should support the achievement of your OKRs and help you create maximum value for yourself and your stakeholders. Spend at least 80% of your time on them—just like I did on my bike trip.

What are your three vital functions? Record them in your logbook.

What percentage of time do you spend today on your vital functions?

What percentage of time should you be spending on them?

Select Your OKRs

You've defined your vital functions. What are the three to five objectives you must achieve to succeed in your role at work or in life? There is a big difference between doing things efficiently and doing things of contribution and significance.

Selecting your objectives is strategic. Forcing yourself to identify and commit to them prevents you from having too many choices. Highly productive people decide on vital objectives that move the needle in their field or role. How could you further move the needle more in your role?

Select 3-5 Objectives

Objectives are the big initiatives.

What is most important for the next three months? Where should you concentrate your efforts? How about for the year?

A two-year study by the Deloitte firm found that "no single factor has more impact than clearly defined goals written down and shared freely... Goals create alignment, clarity and job satisfaction."[67]

Usually they take a quarter to complete, but sometimes a year or longer. You are probably familiar with the SMART goal concept: Specific, Measurable, Achievable, Realistic, and Timely. Think of your objectives as the top three to no more than five SMART goals—the ones that really make a difference. It's important to limit your objectives to three to five—the fewer, the better. Why? Because too many goals dilute your efforts. If you wrap up objectives, you'll have no problem adding another. Focus on the less, and then obsess.

Breakdown Your Objectives into Key Results

Like Climbing a Staircase One Step at a Time

As you finalize your objectives, take a look at your vital functions again. Do your vital functions and the time allocation of 80-90% of your working time on the vital functions contribute to the meeting of your objectives? Are they the "right stuff?" If not, adjust your vital functions. As companies grow, as the context changes, as your job grows in contribution, your vital functions will change, too. So make sure you've invested and committed to the right vital functions that will help you meet your strategic initiatives—the objectives.

> *"If you have more than three priorities (objectives), you don't have any."*
> Jim Collins

Now, there are two kinds of objectives. Going back to the bike trip example, I had "do-able" objectives each day of riding at least eighty miles. That's a *committed* objective. I made a promise to myself I wasn't getting off that bike until I met my committed objective. The probability of meeting your committed goal should be good—if you push and work hard. It shouldn't be a slam dunk, but with effort and putting in your miles, you should see success. So the committed objective is the first type of objective.

The second type of objective, a "stretch" objective, is also known as an aspirational objective. Aspirational goals are shooting for greatness. Think of it as shooting for the moon. Put the achievement of aspirational objectives together day-after-day, and in time, looking back, you'll have accomplished something pretty amazing, far more than you ever believed you could. Even if you shoot for the moon and don't quite make it, you will have landed in the stars. That's pretty good.

How do you know if your aspirational goal is enough of a "stretch"? My definition is that you should be able to hit it 70% of the time. Using the bike ride example again, I knew I had to ride every day to get to Florida. I had to sustain myself—it wasn't a one-day, "one-and-done" ride. If I faced heavy head winds, bad pavement, high heat and humidity, or felt fatigued, did it make sense for me to push as hard as I could to hit my aspirational goal, potentially driving myself to the point of exhaustion? My answer was no. Do the best you can, accept your best efforts, and live to fight another day. Seven out of ten days you'll meet the aspirational goal. That adds up to something very worthwhile. That's excellent performance.

Build a Parking Lot
After you've landed on your objectives, you'll still have new ideas for goals and projects. Some will be really good ideas. Without a doubt, shiny new things and great possibilities will come your way. Don't let them seduce you. Don't start on "side projects" and dilute your efforts. Over the long haul, you'll get far more done by working on your objectives sequentially rather than haphazardly.

When one of these great ideas comes to mind, make a page in your logbook titled "Parking Lot" and list your good ideas. Then review it at the end of the quarter. As you are evaluating your objectives for the next cycle, the idea will have been captured, and you can evaluate it for inclusion. Then, if it passes muster, you'll be able to give it focus and energy.

Choose Your Big Rocks Daily
Every day ask yourself, "WTF?"

I want WTF to become your favorite acronym when you need to turbocharge your productivity. What does WTF stand for? Probably not what you may think it might!

It's "What's the Focus?"

So, what is your focus when it's time to execute on your objectives and corresponding key results? Your focus should be the "Big Rocks."

Each day, you set and crank on your big rocks. Get a succession of big rocks done, and you will accomplish your key result. Eventually, you will accomplish your objective, too.

What's the best way to create your big rocks? When you plan your daily production schedule.

The best way to plan using an OKR system is quarterly, monthly, weekly, and daily.

"Planning is bringing the future into the present so that you can do something about it now."
Alan Lakein

I like to create the next quarter's OKRs with a week or two to go in the calendar quarter. What should your OKRs be for the next 90 days? I invest one to two hours mapping out the upcoming quarter and figuring out my objectives and desired key results. If you've completed, or are nearing completion on an OKR or two, what others should be added? Reviewing your calendar of the past ninety days, how have you invested your precious, valuable time? What percentage of your time has been allocated to your vital functions in pursuit of your OKRs? Has it been eighty to ninety percent? If not, what adjustments must you make? What must you start saying "no" to?

Each month, do a quick review of the previous month. Did you win the month? Why or why not? Where do changes need to be made? What do you need to stop? What must happen so that you make this month happy, productive, and successful? It may be useful to draw four or five boxes, each one representing one week, and to identify your three OKRs and corresponding big rocks to focus on in the upcoming weeks. Do you have new ideas for new initiatives? Do you have some shiny, new, bright ideas? Don't be tempted. Shiny things go into the parking lot. Review your parking lot items each quarter to determine if they have the meddle to become a full-fledged objective or key result.

I prefer preparing my weekly planner early on Sunday mornings for 30 to 45 minutes. It takes out any angst about returning to work on Monday. Review the previous week's activities and results. Did you win the week? Which days did you win? When you see you've made progress on your OKRs, it raises your satisfaction and commitment to reinvention.

After I've created the weekly planner, I make certain my calendar is time-blocked for the upcoming week for my OKRs and corresponding big rocks.

Then I can enjoy a full Sunday with family and friends, knowing I've got a good plan for the week ahead. I review the OKRs and chunk them down for the upcoming week by big rock. Like climbing a staircase, proceed one step at a time. It's my weekly work plan—the weekly planner.

Each day, before you finish your work for the day, identify the big rocks to be completed the following day to make progress on your OKRs. Make calendar adjustments as needed. This is your daily production schedule. You'll review your daily production schedule and big rocks for the day as part of your morning routine the next day. Research says the act of constructing your goals in concrete terms and writing them down makes you 50% more likely to attain them, and 32% more likely to feel in control of your life.

Each day, you tackle the highest impact big rock first. For the first sprint of the day, swallow the big frog, your highest-impact, #1 top priority.

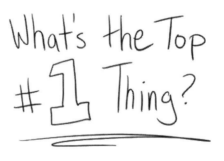

What's the Top #1 Thing?

Get in the habit of writing up your daily production schedule—just like it's used at the factory. Why do you need the daily production schedule? Because you produce! You execute. You are a massive value creator.

You've got your OKRs ready.

Now a few tips to put jet fuel into your production level. Put these tips into place and you'll be glad you did. They are: Just Say "No!"; Plan to Win; Schedule Your Greatness; and Run Sprints, Not Marathons.

Just Say "NO!"
A lot!

Say it more than you are comfortable. A popular myth is that we should say "Yes." We don't want to hurt people's feelings. But when we say "Yes" to one thing, we say "No" to another.

When you are committed to the OKR productivity system, you'll have to say "No"—a lot! Saying "No!" keeps you focused. You may gain 30% or more of your time back by focusing only on what is critical. There is a difference between "interesting things" and deepening your focus on the few things that really matter. Say "No!" to 20-30% more things.

> *"The difference between successful people and very successful people is that very successful people say no to almost everything."*
> Warren Buffett

Given how you've been spending your time, and now considering your newly defined vital functions, OKRs, and the big rocks, what do you need to stop doing?

"We spend a lot of time teaching leaders what to do. We don't spend enough time teaching leaders what to stop. Half the leaders I have met don't need to learn what to do. They need to learn what to stop."

— Peter Drucker

To operate with three objectives means you'll have to learn to say "No" to all the invitations, intriguing projects, and other requests that don't advance your objectives. You need to keep yourself from doing what you shouldn't. When in doubt, say "No."

In Peter Drucker's *The Effective Executive,* he explains: "The executive who wants to be effective and who wants his organization to have effective polices for all programs, all activities, all tasks, always asks: 'Is this still worth doing?' And if it isn't, he gets rid of it so as to be able to concentrate on the new tasks that, if done with excellence, will really make a difference in the results of his own job and in the performance of his organization."[68]

Jim Collins, author of *Good to Great,* did an exhaustive study of companies that turned themselves around going from disappointments to huge successes. What he found was that most of the big changes they made weren't about new initiatives but about the bad things they needed to stop doing.[69]

What must stop at your company and in your area of responsibility? What must you say "No" to?

Look at your calendar for the last month. What should you have said "No" to? How about your calendar for tomorrow and the next week? What should you say "No" to?

Saying "No" and stopping is critical to increasing your productivity. Identify and list at least ten practices, meetings, reports, activities, habits, etc., you must stop doing. You delegate these responsibilities to someone else, outsource them, automate them, or do without them altogether. They are lower-value activities.

At least quarterly, reflecting on your vital few functions and OKRs. Make sure you also review how you've allocated your time. Does your calendar reflect your vital few functions and objectives? Ask yourself, "Where have I spent my time?"

What must you stop doing?

What can you delegate to others? You can't delegate that project or responsibility? Oh, really? No one else can possibly do it as well as you do it? You need humility. When you delegate, it's an epiphany. It's liberating.

How do you to stay focused? You become a *Quitter!* When you start up a business, you do everything. Gradually quit. It frees up time to do the vital functions and objectives. Closely track your progress on the objectives.

Scheduling Your Greatness

Just about everyone who seeks to live a more productive life has a project plan or a to-do list. It's good to get the important things that must be done listed, no doubt about it. Yet for most people, that's where things stop. You try to get your never-ending to-do list completed, only to add more items as thoughts enter your head. What happens?

The list doesn't get done. Distractions set in and time runs out because life happens. And you feel miserable that you've let yourself down. Maybe you lay off the to-do list for a while. But then you feel adrift, knowing there are things "out there" that must be done. But there is no inventory of what needs to be done and by when. You just have a lot of thoughts racing through your brain, and your anxiety level goes on full alert.

No more. From this day forward, I invite you to see to-do lists as evil. Why are they evil? Because if you don't build into your calendar your top priorities – your OKRs and corresponding big rocks – you'll never get everything done. You'll be grinding your gears and that will just lead to discouragement, not empowerment. Each week, schedule your OKRs into your calendar. Look at your calendar. How do you spend your time? Your calendar reveals your true priorities.

This works for free time and training time, too. Those who control their calendars, and stay mindful of investments in time, stay energized. Losing control of your calendar leads to burnout.

Controlling your calendar gives you the time to focus on your greatness so you can do the meaningful, deep work that leads to great productivity.

You schedule quitting time first and work backward from there. Then you'll know how many hours you have. Slot in what needs to get done by priority. This is called "fixed schedule productivity." You need boundaries if you seek work-life balance. This will force you to be more efficient.

Prioritize your time-blocking as follows:
1. Time block your time off away from work;
2. Time block your three OKRs; and
3. Time block your planning time.

"The key is not to prioritize what's on your schedule, but to schedule your priorities."
— Stephen Covey

Run Sprints, not Marathons

Those living a purposeful life break the marathon paradigm for themselves. They know the key to greater productivity and higher performance is to think of the day as a series of sprints. They see each nearby finish line, and they go all-out to reach it knowing they'll have time to rest and renew before the next sprint.

In business and creative work, using the sprinter's approach leads to greater productivity. Elite world-class performers apply the sprinter's approach: concert violinists, Olympic athletes, and entertainers. Here's how.

As they schedule their day, they book two or three 60-minute blocks of "sprint" time. Schedule your block time in hour bursts. An hour is about the maximum time you can go with full concentration and focus. During these blocks, you concentrate on the task at hand—and you produce. The concert pianist practices his score deliberately for a set time. Similarly, you create a bubble of silence, so you can do intentional, concentrated work.

First, you clear the deck. Set the timer on your smartphone for 50 minutes. Then turn off the ringer. You work on the most important task until it's done or the alarm rings.

During your sprint, there are many things you could be doing. Ignore all the things you could do. Not all things matter equally. You've identified the top thing that matters most. Your #1. Sprints put you in position to get what you want done.

Set yourself up for success. Make sure you've got water to stay hydrated and a light snack like baby carrots or nuts if you need.

Remember when you've had successful, productive sprints in the past? Close your eyes and relive those for 30 seconds. How did you feel when you succeeded? You felt focused. Accomplished. Confident. Optimistic.

Feel those emotions again. Feel how good it is to succeed. Remember how good you felt about yourself and your accomplishment. These emotions are triggers for making the upcoming sprint successful and productive. Visualize an awesome sprint for the next hour.

You are narrowly focused. This is a tight, intense focus. For 50 minutes, attack one project or big rock at a time.

You then take 10 minutes to release and recharge. Go for a walk, hydrate, listen to music, do some light exercise, meditate, or grab a healthy snack. Do what prepares you for whatever comes next. Expend energy, then release, renew, and rejuvenate.

Time-block and schedule at least two daily sprints, but ideally three or four. Can you block 50% of your time—four hours? Do your best to do this. Make your sprints as early in your day as possible.

Time-blocks are non-negotiable. Do sprints every single day. It's your responsibility to train people around you—including your boss. This time is critical for your best work. Sprints are your jet fuel for productivity.

Think of your sprint as a 50/10 solution for productivity. It's a 50-minute sprint, followed by a 10-minute break to release, renew, and recharge.

You've planned, you're focused, now you execute.

You must not let trivial tasks or the noise of the world distract you from your priorities. Separate yourself from the world. Turn off all information inputs that tear you away from your precious time and creativity. There are so many tugs and pulls that suck you into the turbulent world and have absolutely nothing to do with your dreams, aspirations, and goals. Focus! Focus! Focus! Now go execute!

Set the timer on your phone for 50 minutes. You've set yourself up with what you need to produce.

"It is those who concentrate on but one thing at a time who advance in this world."
– Og Mandino

Now, it's up to you to concentrate and execute. Do your deep work. Just like I did during my ride from Chicago to Florida, you pedal and put in the miles.

Fifty minutes of intense concentration and deep work consumes a lot of energy. While the brain is only 2% of your body weight, it consumes between 20-25% of the body's oxygen and energy supply.

After your alarm, take five minutes to release. It's like mentally clearing the calculator or cleaning the desk. Breathe, hydrate, move around, and walk.

Then take the five minutes after that to visualize success for your next hour. You might do this while recharging. Maybe go for a quick walk or listen to some upbeat music. Or engage in some light exercise using a resistance band. Visualize how you want to show up. Visualize your interactions with others. Visualize your hope and strategy for ensuring a favorable outcome during the next hour. You are going into the next hour with great intention, whether it is a meeting with colleagues, a sales call, another sprint, or a meal with your family or friends.

In summary, *turbocharging your productivity* is about concentrating on less so that you can accomplish more. If you focus on everything, you focus on nothing. Get laser-like focused on your objectives and the vital functions to meet them. Use the OKR system. Follow the tips. Watch your productivity soar, giving you the time, energy, and resources you need to live the life you desire.

Chapter 6: Pull It All Together

I f you were having a house constructed, you'd likely have an architect draw a blueprint that would serve as the plan, the guide, for the building of your home. Wouldn't it be good to create a blueprint for your life of impact, too?

You've reflected and recorded your thoughts in your logbook. Those responses, reflections, and creations are the ingredients—the raw materials—you'll need to create your impact story and plan. This is the chapter where you pull it all together.

Remember, you are either getting better or getting worse. There is no standing still. The world is changing and so must change too. Young or old, change is a must for you. You can change at any age. Become a better version of you. Reinvent where you must.

But not everyone thinks they need to reinvent themselves.

A very smart and successful man doubts you can.

> *"People over forty-five basically die in terms of new ideas."*
> Vinod Khosla

Vinod Khosla is a billionaire, the co-founder of Sun Microsystems and the founder of Khosla Ventures, a venture capital firm. He is a highly-accomplished man.

What do you think about Khosla's proclamation?

Here's what I think about Khosla's comment. It's BS! It's absolutely not true!

As you've read this book and completed your work in your logbook, you've created new ideas about reinventing your impactful life.

Throughout the book, we've learned of many examples of people—those over forty-five and those under forty-five—who've had new ideas about how they wanted to live in the present and in the future. They've chased those purposes and dreams, and they are creating an impact.

Many have taken this journey. Nothing and nobody is going to stop you. Let's finish up this chapter strong by creating your impact story and plan so that you become unstoppable. I'm betting on you!

Become unstoppable like three people you'll read about in the following pages: Diana Nyad, Terry Hitchcock, and Casey O'Brien.

"Find a Way!"

It's not everyone who has a dream at twenty-eight that gets fulfilled at age sixty-four. Fueled by passion to do what no one had ever done, endurance maverick Diana Nyad committed herself to fulfilling that dream after putting it on hold for three decades.

When she was twenty-five, she became the first person to swim thirty-two miles across Lake Ontario against the current. The next year, she swam twenty-eight miles around the island of Manhattan and made the front page of the *New York Times.*

She next attempted to swim from Cuba to Florida. She failed. Then two days before her thirtieth birthday, she swam a world-record-breaking one hundred three miles from Bimini, The Bahamas, to Jupiter, FL, in what she called her "last competitive swim." She toweled herself after that swim, got dressed, and didn't swim again for thirty years.[70]

She was out of the water for three decades but still had this dream to swim from Cuba to Florida. At age sixty, she committed herself to training. Then two weeks before her sixty-second birthday, after logging hundreds of miles during swimming sessions lasting twelve, fourteen, and even twenty-four hours, she was ready to try the treacherous swim from Havana to Key West. If successful, she would be the first person to swim the distance without a protective shark cage. Unfortunately, rough seas, jellyfish stings, and an injured shoulder aborted that attempt. She tried again and jellyfish stings, a lightning storm, and an asthma attack thwarted that effort.

Two years later, at age sixty-four, she attempted the Cuba to Florida swim once again. Wearing a thin specially designed suit meant to protect her against jellyfish and a customized mask to prevent jellyfish stings to her tongue, she swam through the treacherous waters of the Straits of Florida, against the currents and eddies of the gulf stream in shark-infested waters.

Along her route, she sang herself songs by Bob Dylan and Neil Young. When the seas were rough, she hummed lullabies to help her nerves calm. She didn't sleep or even stop while covering the one hundred ten-mile distance. She just never gave up.

She became the first person to complete the swim from Cuba to Florida without the protection of a shark cage—and she did it in fifty-two hours and fifty-four minutes. During her ultramarathon swim, she made over two hundred thousand strokes. Throughout her swim, she repeated her declaration: "Left hand, I push Cuba back. Right hand, I push forward to Florida."

She had a few messages as she staggered on to the shore at Key West, barely able to walk, and her face and lips swollen with salt. She was hardly able to speak. "One, we should never, ever give up," she said. "Two, you are never too old to chase your dreams. Three. It looks like a solitary sport, but it's a team effort [giving credit to her support crew and staff who accompanied her by boat and kayak]."

Interviewed later, Diana said, "I remember coming out and seeing the faces of the crowd on the beach just so emotionally wrought. I realized afterwards, they weren't weeping because somebody finally made it or somebody set some sports record. They were weeping because they saw someone who refused to give up. And everyone has experienced that, whether it's fighting cancer or raising a difficult child or whatever. Whatever the challenge, it is about resisting pain, managing energy, and having a steel-trap mind to be able to withstand it."

Diana said, "I think a lot of people in our country have gotten depressed, pinned in, pinned down with living lives they don't want. It doesn't have to be that way. You tell me what your dreams are. What are you chasing? It's not impossible!"[71]

She now has a new purpose to get people healthy and moving. She's aiming to inspire a million people to become dedicated "EverWalkers," to walk, get out into the magnificent outdoors and leave the screens that dominate so much of our time.

Diana Nyad had a passion to do something no one had ever done. She never gave up. It took over thirty-five grueling years and five life-and-death attempts to finally become the first individual in history to swim the nearly one hundred eleven miles between Havana and Key West.

Find your purpose. Commit yourself. Stay passionate. Never give up. You are never too old to chase your dreams and fulfill your purpose.

Never, ever give up!

Let's play the long game. While you can make excellent strides in one year, when you play the long game you focus on long-term impact. 2020 marks the start of a new decade. 2030 will be a new decade, and that's not so far away. Think back to where you were and what you were doing in 2010. For me, it seems like yesterday. That's what 2020 will look like in 2030. It will be here before you know it. And those ten years are coming, one way or another, whether you like it or not. So embrace it. Make it the best decade ever, where you will create greater impact than ever before. To operate at your best. Focus on where you want to be in ten years. With a new decade, create a ten-year plan that will be your story and blueprint for creating world-class impact. What will be your plan and declaration for the decade?

Does that mean you won't have wins for ten years? The answer is no. You will. But you're playing the long game. You're not limiting yourself to a short-term flash. You'll get better and better, and you'll create more impact, year after year. What a journey it will be!

Where do you want to see yourself at the end of the decade?

What do you want out of life?

How would you describe yourself and your character in ten years?

How do you want others to describe you and your character in ten years?

A fun way to brainstorm these questions is by making yourself "the person of the decade."

Make Yourself the Time Magazine *'Person of the Decade'*

Let's project you ten years into the future—one decade from today. Imagine that the future you've dreamed for yourself has come to pass. As a matter of fact, you've reinvented yourself to such an impressive extent you have been named *Time's Person of the Decade.*

"I dream my painting, and then I paint my dreams."
Vincent Van Gogh

With your vision and impact plan in place, you can begin "painting" your next decade, just like Van Gogh painted his dreams.

Knowledge and information alone is not what make you operate with impact. Planning is required. Action and execution are required. Make your declaration. Now is the most exciting time to be alive. In ten years, you'll be living 100% purposefully and passionately, leveraging your gifts, strengths, and values, to create impact.

Remember Jack Morgan, our president friend whose situation was our opening story of the book? His impact story may be useful as an example to you as you prepare to craft yours. You can read his impact story in Appendix 4: *Doing Well by Doing Good!*

After you've reviewed Jack Morgan's story, how about setting the timer on your phone for fifty minutes and imagine how your article would read? Grab your logbook and write as fast as you can. If you'd rather use a special interest magazine example that profiles you, and that resonates with you more than *Time*, feel free to choose that one.

Use the following questions as your guide. Your job is to write the key points for each question. You will have created an outline to draft the article. Then you can go back and write the article. Go back to the content you created in your logbook, as that is good material for your article.

If relaxing classical music or smooth jazz helps you reflect, turn it on. Take a few deep breaths to calm your mind and body.

Consider the questions you've reflected on and answered in your logbook from the other chapters. Pull those answers out to use as appropriate.

What is success to you?

What is your purpose from this moment forward?

What are the passions that fuel your purpose? What old passions have stayed with you? Which new passions have you developed? What have you committed to that became a passion?

How did you strengthen your relationships with the people you love the most?

Reviewing each key area in the Wheel of Life. What is the state of each area? What does your life look like in each of these key areas? They are: Health and Fitness, Spirituality, Partner, Career, Family, Friends, Financial, and Fun.

How did you recraft your role to create greater purpose, passion and greater value? How did that work? How were your stakeholders affected?

What helped you turbocharge your productivity?

What were the results of your increased productivity?

What does your daily routine look like? Your morning and evening routines?

Who did you have to become to achieve this success? What kind of character, what kind of mindset, what kind of philosophy did you develop? What kind of walk and talk? What did you have to learn? How did you need to show up, interact with and influence others?

How did you continue to learn, grow, and reinvent?

What did you create and contribute?

What was your impact plan?

What was your impact declaration?

What's the impact you've created?

What were the obstacles you overcame? How did you overcome them?

What are your family and friends saying about your amazing decade?

What about your clients and customers?

If applicable, what are your boss and co-workers saying about your decade and the impact you've created?

As you reflect back on the ten years, how do you feel? What are you proudest of?

Who and how many people did you teach and encourage to reinvent their impact? What were their results?

What did you do that you had always wanted to try but were too afraid in the past to attempt?

What else does the article say about you?

This becomes your impact story for the future. Write your *Person of the Decade* article. Tell yourself that you can make it happen, one day at a time. It replaces the old story you've been telling yourself. Is that old story the one that will get you where you want to go? If it isn't, then it's time to let that story go and replace it with your new impact story.

This is your impact story. Make it your best life story—the one you have to live. You can make it happen because nothing is impossible.

"Nothing is Impossible!"

Terry and Sue Hitchcock met in college and they married shortly thereafter. They have enjoyed the classic American Dream. Living in suburban Minneapolis, Terry worked as an executive and Sue stayed home to manage the household. By their mid-forties, they were happy, in love, and busy raising three children.

Then the unthinkable happened. Sue received a diagnosis of breast cancer. Sadly, the spread of the cancer was aggressive and her treatment was unsuccessful. Sue passed away mere months after her diagnosis.

After Sue died, Terry was thrust into single parenthood—cooking, clothing, and caring for his three young kids. Three days later, Terry lost his job and income.

Times were tough. And Terry's eyes were opened to the plight of single parents. Finally, twelve years after Sue's passing, he had to do something.

It was 1996, and at age fifty-seven, Terry didn't recognize the old man in the mirror anymore. His fire was gone.

He wasn't what you'd call athletic. But he used to challenge himself by entering the local 5K every year. He always came in last. And six months after having a heart attack, and never having run more than this annual 5K, Terry Hitchcock made a decision that would change his life forever.

He got the idea from a Canadian man—Terry Fox, a man who lost his leg to cancer and did something extraordinary in 1980.

This young nineteen-year old decided that what he was going to do was to attempt to run from east to west, across Canada, to raise money for cancer research. After one hundred forty-three days of running, and almost thirty-five hundred miles across Canada (24.5

miles a day), Terry had to leave the highway because the cancer that had taken his leg was now in his lungs. Throughout his run, he raised over twenty-four million dollars to combat cancer. Terry passed away some eight months later. To date, his foundation has raised close to one billion dollars for cancer research.

Inspired by Terry Fox, Terry Hitchcock decided to honor Sue and shine a light on the struggles that thirty-five million American single parents and their children experience. Hitchcock decided to run again. He wasn't going to go on just any run. He wanted to go on a two-thousand-mile odyssey from St. Paul to the Olympic Games in Atlanta![72]

Terry commented, "I knew that the Olympics were going to be held in Atlanta and two of my three children were born there. The Olympics represent going beyond and doing the impossible. I thought, 'Well maybe what I could do is run toward Atlanta and maybe do the equivalent of at least a marathon a day. I think I'll run to the opening ceremonies of the Olympics.' Since I'm a dreamer, I could tell the story of what I'm doing and help raise awareness for single parents and their children."

"No runner that I ever met said that I could do this," Terry said. "They would say it was humanly impossible. Every doctor said, 'You just can't do this,' because while I was training, I had a heart attack halfway through. My cardiologist said, 'Don't do this. You won't live to tell your story.' So all those things were against me, but I just felt with my own faith that this was something I should do—that when I completed it, it's a story for the ages.'"

Despite the odds, Terry hit the streets running with a small team of friends and family. Soon enough he realized just how difficult the journey would be.

His plan was to run slowly, but for a long time, about eight hours a day. Yet when he finally set off he wasn't prepared for the pain-filled realities of running the road.

177

Terry reported, "First of all, the pounding that you put your body through is incredible. Halfway down to Atlanta, both my ankles were fractured and my left kneecap also had a fracture. I was in pain every day and just had to learn to bear it and run above it."

He thought about quitting each and every day. "Actually, it was probably many times during a day. It was very hard." And it only got harder as I ran farther south into warmer temperatures. "

Worst yet, after thirty days of running, his team began to disband. "Five of the six said, 'We're going to go home,' because it wasn't fun. It was very hard work. They were young and they missed their friends. The thirty-first day I'm standing on the side of the road with a trailer going home, and beside me is my oldest son Christian. He is looking at me saying, 'Dad, I'm not going to leave you.' It seemed like Chris and I against the world."

"Crossing the finish line at Centennial Park in Atlanta, knowing that I had just finished almost twenty-one hundred miles—and I was still alive—that made it all worth it."

Terry's run required running slightly over a marathon a day for seventy-five days—an average of twenty-eight miles per day.

It has shown me, in no uncertain terms, that I am here on this earth to 'teach,' to show others that their 'daily marathons' are possible to get through each day, that nothing is really impossible, that one's own personal faith is the strength we all need to help run our marathons, and that I am simply a vehicle to make a difference for others.

Terry Hitchcock's purpose is this: *I am here on this earth to show others that their daily marathons are possible to get through each day and that nothing is really impossible.*

Years after his run, the late producer and director Tim Vandesteeg completed a documentary called *My Run*, narrated by Academy

Award winner Billy Bob Thornton. *My Run* won 10 awards. Hitchcock also wrote a book telling his story, *A Father's Odyssey.*[73]

The story of Terry Hitchcock is more than a story about a man running multiple marathons; it's about the daily marathons every one of us runs.

When you're faced with obstacles, you have a choice.

If a fifty-seven-year-old man with no athletic ability can run a marathon a day for seventy-five consecutive days, then just imagine what you can do!
You can give up or you can keep pushing. It's your decision.

As Terry Hitchcock shows, "Nothing is impossible."

Overcome the Inevitable Resistance

Terry Hitchcock faced an almost insurmountable amount of resistance on his run. But he overcame the resistance. You must, too.

While comfort is the villain that seeks to stop you from living a purposeful life, so is its evil cousin resistance, which targets you once you've committed to living a life of impact. As you've chosen to get off the couch of the comfortable life for a life of impact, resistance hates that declaration and will try to destroy your dreams.

Resistance is a most powerful force. It is invested in the status quo and will work tirelessly to sabotage your efforts to live purposefully. Your ego relies on the status quo to keep you from becoming the person you aspire to become. Human nature fights like hell to prevent change. Resistance tries to prevent you from achieving the grandest vision of yourself. It's insidious and it can plague you forever.

Its weapons are formidable. It will seed you with self-doubt that can lead to passivity and self-sabotage. It will try to strip you of your motivation. It may delude you into thinking you can't make your new impact story come alive – that what has happened in the past will continue indefinitely. It will try to persuade you that reinvention is too hard or that it will take too long. Or maybe you'll try it halfheartedly, lose your enthusiasm, and then claim it just doesn't work. It will encourage you to procrastinate. And it can derail you in many other ways: through negative self-talk, addictions, cynicism, distractions, and the fear of failure—even the fear of success.

If you have a bad day, or a string of bad days, resistance will shame you to quit. Resistance is going to happen. It's good to plan for it now. When you have a rough day, or a series of bad days, or weeks or more, frame your challenge in a more positive light, like you would for a good friend. Instead of beating yourself up, be compassionate with yourself. Acknowledge your flaws. It's okay — you're human too. Remember, there are exciting opportunities down the road for you to live on purpose and create impact. Positively reframe this little setback, using motivating self-talk and a commitment to double down on your impact plan, just like you were consoling a good friend.

What will be your distractions and excuses? List them in your logbook. If you let them get in your way, you'll face the same limitations you always have. Don't surrender your power!

How will you overcome resistance? You overcome by believing in the deepest way possible, with every fiber of your body, in your purpose, your definition of success, and your impact story as *Person of the Decade.* You overcome by committing to the flourishing person you seek to become. And you overcome by creating and living by a routine that overwhelms resistance.

It takes self-discipline. Resistance hates habits, routines, structure, and concentration. Reinvention requires skill and will. Now you know the skill. It's up to you to muster the will. Reinventing your impact is mostly will. Have the courage to do this, to do more, and to be more. Be unstoppable. Terry Hitchcock overcame resistance. He was unstoppable.

Which pain will you choose? The pain of discipline or the pain of regret?

– Jim Rohn

Reinvention is forever. It is an on-going process. It's never completed. Make it impossible for resistance to sabotage you, like Casey O'Brien has done.

Wake Up! Kickass! Repeat!

Casey O'Brien is a nineteen-year old man you have likely never heard of. He's a redshirt sophomore at the University of Minnesota (a collegiate athlete in his second year of eligibility). Casey plays football under head coach PJ Fleck for the Golden Gophers, and his only action on the gridiron has been for a few extra point attempts. Yet his story is quite remarkable. He's a man who's having an impact.

When Casey was thirteen, a freshman at Cretin-Derham High School in St. Paul, his life revolved around sports. He was a quarterback on the football team when he began experiencing intense pain in his left knee for no apparent reason.

Several doctors checked out Casey's knee and none could identify the problem. His grandfather told him that if he chose to play football, he could expect that his knees would always ache. But Casey knew his body and knew his pain was more than the typical football grind.

His parents took him to the University of Minnesota Children's Masonic Hospital for an examination. There, he was diagnosed with a very serious disease, osteosarcoma, an extremely rare form of bone cancer. Doctors removed a softball size tumor from his knee, removed all the cartilage and replaced his knee. They said his football career was over.

But Casey refused to quit. He had to get back on that football field. He said, "Cancer has taken over. I want my life back. I want to play football again." And he created a plan to resume playing football.

He completed his chemotherapy. He conditioned himself and worked tirelessly. Acknowledging his quarterbacking days were behind him, he switched positions to placeholder. Casey created a declaration, a visual commitment of his pledge to get back on the football field. This was his impact declaration, a simple hand painted sign he posted in his bedroom. It read:

"Wake up! Kickass! Repeat!"

In 2015, Casey's junior year of high school, the cancer came back, this time with spots on both lungs. He underwent more surgeries and more chemo. Casey battled back and refused to quit. In his junior year, he overcame a third bout of cancer. Eight days after a long surgery, sixty stitches in his lung and two broken ribs, Casey played in a sectional tournament game as placeholder. The next day, he went to chemotherapy.

Fast forward to 2017. Fourteen surgeries and several treatments of chemotherapy later, Casey has graduated and enrolled at Minnesota, the only FBS (Football Bowl Subdivision of the NCAA) team in the country that gave him a medical clearance. Coach Fleck gave Casey a shot. Casey told Coach Fleck, "I came here to play, not to stand on the sideline."

In January 2018, the cancer came back a fourth time. Casey had lung surgery, but didn't miss a single spring practice in March. Casey beat cancer again. All told, since 2013, Casey spent three hundred nights at the University of Minnesota Children's Masonic Hospital. Today, he spends his days there as a visitor, and he offers the young patients and their families a reminder of what is possible. He says to listen to the doctors and staff because they are the people who will carry you through. He tells them to never give up hope. In Casey's words, "Never give up!"

Casey shares his story, that devastating news, the circumstances he was placed in—these things were not going to dictate his life and his behavior. He wanted to play football again and he wasn't going to take no for an answer.

On July 19, 2019, Casey delivered the keynote speech at the Big 10 Football Kickoff Luncheon in Chicago. He shared the memory of the call from his childhood hero, former Gopher and NFL great Eric Decker, when he had learned of Casey's cancer challenge in 2015. Decker told him, "Stay strong and never give up. You have the whole world behind you." It reminded Casey that simple words can be the most encouraging.[74]

Competing for a starting job behind two redshirt seniors, Casey got his chance during the 2019 season. He debuted on October 19, when he held two extra points in the Gophers victory at Rutgers. As Coach Fleck described Casey to the team in presenting the game ball that afternoon in the victorious locker room, "We have a living angel with us, men. He has played Big 10 football, something no one can take away from him. He's defeated cancer four times. He's rowing the boat with us. That's Casey O'Brien."[75]

On November 25, Casey posted on Instagram that he needed surgery for a spot on one of his lungs. He had the surgery, and he is currently undergoing treatment. His prognosis is good. It looks like Casey has beaten cancer the fifth time. In Atlanta on December 12, Casey was awarded the Disney Spirit Award, live on ESPN, presented annually to college football's most inspirational player.[76]

While not cleared medically to fly, Casey and his family made the long car trip to Orlando where they watched the Gophers beat Auburn 31-24 in the Outback Bowl on New Year's Day.

Watch for Casey to be back for the 2020-2021 season. Who would bet against him? He'll never quit. As we know, he'll "Wake up! Kickass! Repeat!" while he encourages others stricken with cancer and other adversities to do the same and never give up!

Your Impact Plan: A Manifesto for Life

In twenty years plus of coaching corporate leaders, I've seen many leaders who have prepared what is called an "individual development plan." Well intentioned and usually sponsored by the HR department, these individual development plans are created typically to address an improvement in needed skills, styles, or behaviors.

In my view, these are rarely ambitious or inspiring plans for positive change. If any growth or development takes place, it is typically marginal improvement. What usually happens is that as commitment of the individual leader begins to fade, the individual development plans just fade away, too, with few results.

The individual development planning process starts again the next year, typically focused on another development need. The program is largely fruitless, year after year. While learning and development is given lip service in many companies, the individual development planning process leaves a lot to be desired for achieving meaningful, lasting growth and change. It's setting the bar so low. It's almost a game—a "check-the-box" kind of exercise. It's become a lame concept—past its sell-by date. It's not nearly a big enough challenge, and it isn't linked to the person's purpose, passions, and the need for growth and reinvention. Consequently, there is usually little commitment of the individual executive to change.

It's time to shift the paradigm. You know you have more potential. You are likely not even close to fulfilling your potential.

If you've committed to living on purpose, to learning, growing, and reinventing to become someone who is #1 in your profession or in an area meaningful to you, who lives a life of impact, wouldn't you commit to creating a blueprint or a plan for becoming your best? You would commission a blueprint for your new house. Isn't your life more valuable than your house? Wouldn't you create a plan for you to fulfill your purpose and life?

You write your impact story and create your impact plan so they become the manifesto for what your life will be all about. This is about living intentionally, purposefully, and with impact.

Your Impact Declaration

Let your impact story become your impact plan – your blueprint. Your impact declaration is your definitive statement of where you are pointing your life over the next decade.

You get to name it, claim it, and frame it. Your impact declaration is your ticket to creating what's possible. You create your own reality. Your declaration reminds and reinforces you, in a brief memorable statement, of the future you are creating during the next ten years.

It should be short. Write down your declaration—a few words are fine. Make it no more than two sentences so you will always remember it. Think of this declaration as the key that unlocks the future you are committed to create. Your declaration has to be bold. No weak declarations or you won't stay committed or create any impact. I want you to make a declaration that's world class.

Think one or, at most, two sentences. It could be:

"I'm going to be the best (fill in the profession or role) I can be! "
Or *"I'm the driving force to improve the healthcare access for all in the USA."*
Or, *"I'm going to be the most powerful, healthiest and fittest woman, wife, and mom ever."*

Terry Hitchcock had his declaration he repeated over and over as he ran the equivalent of seventy-five marathons in a row. *"Nothing is Impossible."*

Diana Nyad used her declaration, *"Left hand, push Cuba back. Right hand, push forward to Florida,"* to battle through the grueling fifty-four-hour swim of 110 miles in the Gulf of Mexico. It kept her going.

As Casey O'Brien beats cancer for the fifth time in six years, he uses his declaration of *"Wake Up! Kickass! Repeat!"* to keep him powerful, strong, and determined.

Frank Pleticha uses his declaration to go out on cold winter nights as he marshals others to join him in the battle to end sex trafficking in Minnesota. *"Not on my watch!"*

Jack Morgan uses his declaration as motivation as he works with industry leaders and politicians, serving those who do not have healthcare insurance or are underserved. *"Do well by doing good – universal healthcare for all!"*

Once you have your declaration, you've simplified your life. Every situation, person or choice that comes your way gets evaluated with a simple question. *"Does this help me live my impact declaration or not?"* You answer with a simple "yes" or "no."

You remove all the distractions. You avoid getting overloaded by unimportant information.

You add things and people who help you meet your impact declaration. You remove—or work around if you cannot entirely remove—those who don't.

You've created a purpose and a vision for yourself that you are going to make happen. You have an impact story that is your blueprint for making it happen. Your impact declaration continuously reminds you of your journey and destination.

Will there be obstacles and aches and pain along the way? You bet. That's life. When life knocks you to the ground, get back up and keep walking. You've identified your destination, so walk, swim, or ride those miles, knowing you'll be leaving blood, sweat, and tears on the trail. That's good. That's what happens.

It's going to happen if you keep going. But it won't happen if you quit. As your coach, I won't quit on you or your dream. Don't you either!

Encourage Others to Create Impact, One Person at a Time

That's my impact declaration. Encourage others to create impact, one person at a time.

It was cemented in my heart when I was quite young, although I didn't know it then.

You see, everyone needs a strong person in their lives, someone who can encourage and believe in you along life's winding road. Particularly after your heart has been broken. I was fortunate to have experienced at a young age how profound the impact can be when strong people encourage and believe in you.

When I was eight years old, my dad died unexpectedly from a heart attack. Over the next five years five other men who I loved died. One each year. My favorite uncle died of a sudden heart attack the year after Dad passed. A year later, my sister-in-law's brother, who was like a big brother to me, died tragically in a car crash at age 19, along with two of his classmates. Only the driver survived. Young men doing stupid stuff with tragic consequences.

My grandpa succumbed to stomach cancer the next year. The uncle I was closest to died at the age of 42 of a massive heart attack the following year on Easter Sunday, leaving a wife and two young daughters behind. The next year, the man who lost his 19-year-old son three years before in the car crash, my sister-in-law's dad, whom we dearly loved, died a death of despair after losing his only son so tragically.

Those years when I was between the ages of eight and 14 were so difficult. I lost Dad, Uncle Bob, Jack, Grandpa, Uncle Rich, and Mr. D. *Six men in six years—men I loved*. All the tears, pain and sorrow. I dreaded those far too frequent visitations and funerals. It was a dark time.

I asked, "Why? Why did I keep losing every man I loved?" I couldn't get answers that made sense. It was a time of despair, anger, and fear, of getting kicked in the teeth by life for no understandable reason. To add to the fear, during this awful period, my only brother was a tank commander in the thick of the action in the Viet Nam War. Late night calls made us jump for the phone. We dreaded the thought of seeing a uniformed officer walking to our front door with more tragic news. It was almost too much to bear.

Here's the deal. Every one of us needs someone who is strong who encourages and believes in us. We all need someone like that in our lives. The person who was there to encourage and believe in me was my mom. She's the one who guided me through this awful chapter and into the person I've become. While I didn't know it at the time, she also shaped my purpose.

What did Mom do? She always showed me encouragement and love. She worked hard to raise me with values that guided my thinking. She was optimistic that things would be better in the future. She taught me to have faith, that God had a plan, and that some tragedies were unexplainable. She taught me that there are always ups and downs in life. These were devastating losses, but she reminded me there would be good moments, too. We needed to get up and do the best we could, to stay strong and adapt, to weather the challenges and have faith for a better tomorrow.

I witnessed firsthand how she handled adversity. She prayed. She had a deep faith. She was optimistic, believing the best was yet to come. And finally, she served. She looked for ways to help others.

A few years after Dad died, Mom moved us from Kentucky to a suburb of Chicago, where her parents lived. They were both in their 80s, and her dad was close to death. They needed her help. Shortly after we arrived, my grandfather passed away.

To support us, Mom got a job as a legal secretary. If it wasn't enough to commute by train each day to and from the city for work, she then cooked and cared for her faltering mom who suffered dementia and raised her rebellious and often angry son.

She dragged me to church, kicking and screaming, and she'd bring little old ladies to our home for Sunday dinner after church. When I was 13, the last thing I wanted to do was hang out on a Sunday afternoon with these old widows in their 70s or 80s. But that's what I did, at least until 3 or 4 pm when I could run out the door and play football, basketball, or baseball at the park.

When I got my driver's license at 16, part of the deal in order to drive Mom's car was to drive the old ladies to our home and then back to their homes. I served as the young chauffer—and at times, unbeknownst to me, the designated driver!

She insisted that I be a gentleman, that I dress in a coat and tie, and that I put my arm out for them to hold and escort them into either our house or theirs. At our small home, I was to open the door for them, take and hang up their coats, offer them a seat, take drink orders, prepare a glass of wine or a drink for them, and pass food when asked. I helped serve the dinner and I listened and contributed to the dinner conversation. I asked polite questions of our guests. I smiled, was kind and courteous, and I helped clean up afterwards. Mom told me that we were lucky to be a "slice of sunshine for people less fortunate than ourselves." At the time, I didn't see it that way!

When I asked her why we always had these ladies over, Mom replied, "When we do this, we help somebody feel a little better about themselves." Mom seemed to find the women whose own families ignored or marginalized them, the ones who seemed like they had nobody to care for them. It was a real-time example of generosity, empathy, and compassion for others. Mom always said, "Just help one person feel a little better about themselves." That was her declaration. I slowly began to understand this was important to her.

Mom reinvented herself from a stay-at-home wife and mom to a single parent, a breadwinner, and a caregiver. To this day, she was the most generous, resilient, and inspiring person I've ever met. She taught me how to care for others and treat people well. These are lessons I use daily.

As a boy and young man, I loved to play baseball. Baseball was my outlet. I loved the competition, of being part of a team. I loved the camaraderie with the guys and the excitement of the game. My love of the game was passed on to me by my Dad and it was nurtured by my mom after his death. I tell the *"Game of Catch"* story in the opening of my book, *The Reinvented Leader*: *Five Steps for Becoming Your Best*. It's also in Appendix D of this book if you would like to read it.

Baseball was my escape. It was a game where an adolescent could channel his rage and testosterone by throwing a baseball as hard as he could. Fortunately, my coach, John LaSage, knowing of my family situation and seeing some potential in the left-arm attached to my tall, gangly body, began to shape me as a pitcher and a ballplayer. He taught me to respect the game. He taught me how to put on and wear the uniform, how to warm up and practice, how to take the field for the game, how to treat teammates, how to handle wins and losses, and how to respect your competition. There was a right way to play the game and a wrong way to play. Coach LaSage taught us the fundamentals of the game and built our baseball skills. But more importantly, he taught us the right way to play the game. He showed me how to become a ballplayer. In three years, by the time I was 15, we went from the worst team to winning the league championship. *He encouraged and believed in me.*

He taught me that if I committed myself, studied, and practiced the right way, that if I stayed open-minded to learning and growing, then good things would happen in my life. Coach LaSage's lessons were a recipe for living a good life.

While in high school I found another sport I became passionate about—skiing. I loved the cold air, the speed, the thrill of skiing straight down the hill without turning, and the risks of pushing yourself to the limits of safety. When I joined the ski club and took that ninety-minute bus ride with other kids to Wilmot Mountain every Saturday in the winter, just over the Wisconsin border, I was hooked. The very first Saturday of ski club it snowed six inches of powder. It felt like gliding on air, skiing in that fresh, light snow. Competing against my friends to prove who could ski the best, who had the courage to take the big jumps, and who could best handle the moguls (those big random bumps that result from ski turns, and which aren't flattened by the grooming machines). Skiing was freedom, exhilaration, and a challenge to become better and better. I dreamed of skiing the mountains in the Rockies and in Europe. Skiing each Saturday was my winter getaway—where I didn't have to think or worry about life.

Skiing also cost money, so it gave me the motivation to cut more lawns in the summer, to shovel snow in the winter, to work as a janitor at the local YMCA, and to umpire Little League baseball games, all to finance my winter passion. Skiing developed my work ethic.

Fast forward a few years. With the encouragement and lessons taught by Mom and the baseball skills and life lessons taught by Coach LaSage, I had a reason to go to college.

Mom encouraged my interests in fields where I could help others. I enjoyed journalism, political science, and public administration courses. I envisioned a career in public service that would make the world a better place. After graduation and working in state government for a few years, I developed an interest in human resources and business. I liked the competition of business, and believed a career in human resources was the best place where I could make people's lives better. I earned an MBA at night. Working in HR, the work I loved most was helping individual leaders and their teams perform at a higher level. As the promotions and bigger jobs came my way, there was less time to do that type of work.

I experienced first-hand the challenges leaders face. The high expectations, the relentless global competition, the competing priorities and the stress to deliver results. I also knew that everyone needed someone who encouraged and believed in them, and often these people were missing in their lives.

Leaders need a trusted advisor who has been there, who sees their potential, who understands them and their situation and can offer wise counsel. Leaders need a trusted advisor with no agenda but to assist them in becoming more successful. A trusted advisor who can help brainstorm strategies, make important introductions, and provide key insights. Someone who can encourage, recognize, and inspire. Someone who can show how to communicate persuasively and influence corporate moguls. Someone who can help them learn, grow and reinvent.

After careful reflection, I committed to pursuing my passion. I left my group vice president of human resources role to start an executive coaching practice where I assist CEOs and c-suite level leaders to become their best and create massive value and impact. I've been blessed to do this purposeful work for twenty years. Through my work experiences and the lessons my clients have taught me, I've been fortunate to write six books where I share with readers how to reinvent their leadership, how to become happier, how to become more productive, and, now, how to live with more purpose and to create greater impact. I love my work.

My life has been blessed in many other ways, too. I have been blessed by my beautiful and talented wife, Mary, and our family. Together we share five adult children, two sons-in-laws and five grandchildren. We refer to our family as the Fabulous Fourteen, and we love spending time together.

For the past ten years, I have been blessed to be part of a small group of eleven Christian men who encourage, uplift, and hold me accountable. Together, we wrote and published a book titled, *Good Men, Great Thoughts: A Daily Devotional*. Sometime ago, when we were exchanging great thoughts, we shared our favorite biblical verses. My favorite is Ephesians 2:10.

For we are God's masterpiece, he has created us anew in Christ Jesus so we can do the good things he planned for us a long time ago.

Ephesians 2:10 resonates with me as I believe everyone is a masterpiece who has many good things they must do. Oftentimes, we need a strong person who encourages and believes in us so we can shine and flourish, to be the spark for the good things that need to be done.

I've learned that the good work that I have been put on earth to do is this – my purpose:
To guide others through the moguls, so they can see what's possible and become unstoppable.

My unique gift is seeing someone's greatness and understanding their situation so that we can brainstorm possibilities and they can act with inspiration, confidence, and commitment.

I'm committed to living a life of impact. As we know, impact is defined as having a strong, powerful effect or influence on a situation or a person.

My impact declaration statement is:

Encourage others to create impact, one person at a time.

While Mom passed away nearly thirty years ago, I believe she would agree that I've followed her declaration: "Just help one person feel a little better about themselves."

By living a life of impact, when we make others feel a little bit better about themselves, we can feel a little better about ourselves, too. Living a life of impact is not just a gift to others and the world, but a gift to ourselves. My hope is that you live a life of impact and encourage and show others how to live this way too. *We need you to live a life of impact.*

> *"Helping one person might not change the world, but it could change the world to one person."* Anonymous

Win the Day

To fulfill your purpose and make an impact, make every day count.

Every day, focus on winning the day. Don't worry about tomorrow. Just win today. You win today, you build momentum, and you achieve what is most important to you.

"To get through the hardest journey we need to take only one step at a time but we must keep on stepping."
— Chinese Proverb

On that exhilarating and exhausting bike trip, when I was sitting in the saddle, I only focused on pedaling to the next town. Just start and then keep pedaling. If I arrived at the town I'd planned the previous night when charting my upcoming ride for the day, I'd met my goal. If I surpassed that town and maybe rode to a few more towns down the road, I hit my stretch big rock. I never worried about the following day's ride. I knew that tomorrow, I'd have six or eight hours to focus on that journey!

Sometimes things didn't go according to plan. Mechanical breakdowns. Inclement weather. Fatigue. I had to work through those obstacles, just like you work through obstacles in your life. Yes, the obstacles were a pain and could turn a challenging ride into a brutal grind at times. You could even let the obstacles make you quit. You know you can't do that!

Here is what the bike trip taught me at age 21: *embrace the grind*!

You work through the grind. Keep pushing. Never quit. One step forward or one pedal push—that's what it takes and you're on your way. Think about Diana Nyad's fifty-four-hour grind. Think about Rachel hiking up those mountains in the Himalayas for thirty-days. Compared to their trips, my bike ride looked like a lap around the block!

Win the day. Come back tomorrow and then win that day. Build a series of winning days and now you've built momentum. You must win the day on your journey, too! And build momentum toward achieving your most important dreams and goals.

Or maybe your job is such that you feel you have no control to go about it differently, or produce differently or to better yourself for the job of your dreams. Maybe you feel stuck.

It's all about choices, isn't it? Are you going to make excuses or demonstrate some bold action that just may change your life for the better? What's your decision?

Everyone has their own story. They are where they are in life. I appreciate that life isn't fair. Life didn't feel fair to me when I was eight years old and my dad unexpectedly and suddenly passed away from a massive heart attack. So, I get it. Life delivers big, crushing blows at times. When this happens to you, you have a choice: to be resilient and overcome the adversity or quit. Never, ever, ever quit.

I don't want you to say, "this won't work for me," and then quit without applying what you've learned. A clear, compelling purpose and vision of the future – your impact story, plan and declaration – that is authentically yours is a most powerful magnet. When you make your purpose and impact a must-do, you can make huge strides and accomplish results you never imagined.

If you are dissatisfied with where you are, what's the necessity that makes you need to move away from that dissatisfaction? Is it for you? Is it for a cause? Is it to be your best? Is it for your children? Is it to break out of the rut or negative situation you are in?

What's the price you pay if you stay stuck where you are?

Once you put your finger on the need for change, and you know there is no staying where you are any longer—that's no longer an option—all of a sudden, it's easier to stay the course. Things start falling into place. You'll win the day. Then another and another. When you are committed and accountable to your purpose and dreams, you will find a way.

What I know is if you quit on yourself or see yourself a victim, doomed to your current circumstances, the world will happily let you stay in your spot. When you argue for your limitations, you get to keep them.

So be accountable to your purpose, your dreams, and your impact story and plan. Ask yourself at the close of each day:

How faithfully did I serve the purpose that is deep inside of me?

If you find yourself still struggling with discipline, it's because of one of three reasons: 1. You haven't made your purpose compelling enough; 2. You haven't owned your role; or 3. You don't have the confidence you can be a success.

Which is it? Decide to get over it. Embrace the discipline. Get the help of a coach. Embrace the grind.

Remember what your grandmother told you as a child, *"Where there's a will, there's a way!"* She was right! You must be accountable to your purpose, dreams, and hopes.

Let's win the day today!

Build Momentum

You will build momentum by stacking together several days that you've won. When this happens, not only will you make progress on your desired goals, but you will also have a sustainable process you can use the rest of your life to shape the future you'd like. Additionally, your self-confidence soars.

Remember when I started that bike trip? I'd never ridden over ten miles on a ride. My guesstimate was that I might be able to ride sixty miles before collapsing due to exhaustion. When I planned my ride and started pushing those pedals, I rode one hundred fifty miles on day one.

Five days later, when I'd ridden over six hundred fifty miles, I knew how to get those miles in to win the day every day. And I intended and expected to get those miles. I had a routine a system that I could rely on to ensure a good ride. Winning the day was my mission. As I got closer to Florida, I looked back from where I'd come and I could see the progress I'd made on my journey. This led to confidence that I could tackle any challenges that came my way.

The planning, focus, and execution of the daily rides turned out to be a routine that had applicability beyond the long bike journey. I won the days and built momentum. Planning, focus, and execution can be applied in any area of your life that you seek to improve or reinvent.

Get a Coach

If you want to have great impact, you can't do it alone.

A great coach brings a new set of lenses to bear. You need advisors, teachers, and accountability partners. Every successful person needs good mentors to help you become the person you desire. With an experienced guide, you'll get there faster, and without as many mistakes.

If a book was all you needed, everyone would have six-pack abs. What you need is training and coaching to help you implement the ideas into your life and business and perform at an elite level.

In 1993, psychologist K. Anders Ericsson published, "The Role of Deliberate Practice in the Acquisition of Expert Performance" in *Psychological Review*. This work debunked the idea that an expert performer was gifted or a prodigy.[77] Instead, Ericsson gave us the first real insights into mastery and birthed the idea of the "10,000-hour rule," which uber-author Malcolm Gladwell popularized in his book *Outliers*. Ericsson found that "the single most important difference between these amateurs and the three groups of elite performers is that the future elite performers seek out teachers and coaches and engaged in supervised training, whereas the amateurs rarely engage in similar types of practice."[78]

What did Mark Phelps, the most decorated Olympic athlete in history with 28 medals, say about his coach, Bob Bowman? "Without my coach, I had no shot at winning the medals." You need an experienced veteran to help you get there.

A coach will help you design and implement your training. Atul Gawande is a surgeon at Brigham and Women's Hospital, a professor of surgery at Harvard Medical School, and a writer for *The New Yorker*. He's also a tennis devotee.

While watching the Wimbledon tennis tournament on television, he saw the Spanish star, Rafael Nadal, being encouraged by his coach. Gawande wondered why he shouldn't have a coach. No senior colleague had observed him in the eight years since he'd established his surgical practice. He had conducted more than 2,000 surgeries in that period. Like most work, medical practice is largely unseen by anyone who might raise one's ability.

So he hired a coach, a retired general surgeon with whom he trained under during his residency. What were the results? His coach observed small things. And it was the small things Gawande had to worry about. Things like draping, the positioning of elbows, lighting, and the choice of instruments. He discussed how he planned to do surgery with his coach. His coached observed and provided feedback. Since taking on the coach, his complication rates have gone down. He feels like he's learning again. He's discovered he needs a coach to do his best work.

"Spending the three or four hours per month has almost certainly added more to my capabilities than anything else," says Gawande. "It's never easy to submit to coaching, especially for those who are well along in their career. Coaching may well be the most effective intervention designed for human performance."[79]

He believes that coaches can help anyone in any profession, especially those that deal with human complexity. Coaching can help anyone master roles that often take years to master – such as being a Fortune 500 CEO. For example, coaching can help you read a room in a tense negotiation, deliver difficult news, or make specific adjustments as needed.

Coaching is a process for achieving results. Those who seek to become their best—athletes, performers, and leaders—all have coaches. Why shouldn't you? Your coach will help you see you as others see you. He will also see you and the company in which you operate with a different set of lenses. That is invaluable to you. You'd be hard pressed to find elite achievers who don't have coaches helping them in key areas of their life.

If you are committed to achieving extraordinary productivity and results, you'll find that a coach gives you the best chance possible. And it's never too soon or too late to get a coach.

When *Fortune* magazine interviewed Eric Schmidt, the former CEO of Google, for its "Best Advice I Ever Got" series,[80] he said:

"Everyone needs a coach."

A great coach has the experience and know-how to help you master what you need to know. A great coach understands and supports your vision of living on purpose and creating great impact. A great coach will bring ideas and will be a brainstorming partner with you. A great coach will help you build the new skills and capabilities you'll need for the journey. A great coach will be honest with you. A great coach will hold you accountable to your commitments. A great coach will celebrate and recognize your efforts and accomplishment along your journey. A great coach will help you reinvent yourself, to help you become your best.

To operate with great impact, do what the other high achievers do from all walks of life: get a coach.

It's Your Time

My job is to help you lead a life of great impact.

We've come a long way together. You've been doing the work. I never said it would be easy, but you stuck with me, read the book, and did the work. I bet you are glad you did!

Now, it's your time to reinvent, to implement your impact plan. Don't settle for "couldas, wouldas, shouldas." Don't let excuses be your legacy. You have the knowledge. You know what to do. Kill the resistance. Get moving.

Change will occur with or without you. Take control and reinvent your future. It's your birthright to be your best! This is your moment to shine. Be the hero of your story of your life.

"Everyone has a supreme destiny."
Oprah

*People who cannot invent
and reinvent themselves
must be content with
borrowed postures, secondhand
ideas, fitting in instead of
standing out.'
— Warren G. Bennis*

Someday, when you stand before your Creator, at the end of your life, how will you answer His questions?

Did you use that gift every day to live a life of purpose?

Were you passionately using your purpose to serve others?

Did you encourage others to find their purpose and live a life of impact?

What was the impact you created?

I believe you are committed to creating impact and achieving your fullest potential.

"The ultimate reason for setting goals is to entice you to become the person it takes to achieve them."
Jim Rohn

How old are you? Multiply your age and 365 and that will give you the number of days you've lived on this planet. As an example, if you are 50 years old, you've lived 18,250 days. Life expectancy in the US is 79 years old. Statistically speaking, you can expect to live another 10,585 days. If you are 60, you've got, on average, 6,935 days left.

Time is ticking. We all know that nothing is promised to us. Commit to living a life of impact and making each day count.

While you will hopefully have many more mornings ahead of you, statistics suggest, on average, you have that many more mornings to wake up. Time is ticking. Get to work, my friend!

How will you live more courageously, with purpose and passion?

How do you feel about how you are spending your most precious currency—time?

How do you feel about the impact you are creating?

What must change?

Now imagine you are eighty years of age. You have lived purposefully and followed your impact story and plan. You've got no regrets or disappointments. You've created great impact.

Your grandchildren ask you, "How did all this happen?" It happened because you answered the call. You had a plan. You put in the miles and you got the training and coaching you needed—that's how it happened.

Or, you missed it. Opportunities passed you by. You knew what to do, but you didn't execute.

What do most people in hospice or at the end of their lives regret the most? They regret not taking the chances to pursue their own dreams. They regret not taking risks and playing their own game. You don't want the future regrets.

What will the 80-year-old you answer?

"This is the true joy in life, the being used for a purpose recognized by yourself as a mighty one; the being thoroughly worn out before

you are thrown on the scrapheap; the being a force of Nature instead of a feverish, selfish little clod of ailments and grievances complaining that the world will not devote itself to making you happy."
George Bernard Shaw

You have to decide now. What's the opportunity that exists when you create great impact? What will you become? What's the price you'll pay if you fail to pursue your opportunity?

It's your time. Your purpose, your passion, and your productivity combine together to create an exponential effect that has the potential to create great impact. Will you seize the potential? Your life, your future, and your best life lie ahead in this next decade. The time is now.

Impact is defined as having a strong, powerful effect or influence on a situation or a person.

And make no mistake about it. You are here to have a *great impact* in this world. You were born to make an impact.

It's for you, your family, your friends, your work colleagues, your followers, and the world. We need you to live with purpose and unleash your great impact. The world needs you to be as impactful as you can be. When you do, you give us hope. And in this crazy, volatile, and uncertain world, isn't that what we all need? Hope?

It's your time!

I look forward to learning about your journey. All the best.

Appendix 1: Calling All CEOs—A Priority Higher Than Profits, Leading with Purpose and Impact

For more than four decades, many of America's influential CEOs have put the needs of their shareholders first—and by a wide margin. They loyally followed Nobel economist Milton Friedman's shareholder primacy theory, "There is one and only one social responsibility of business, to engage in activities designed to increase its profits." In short, they see the CEO's job as to make money for shareholders.

In today's world, characterized by a deepening distrust of business, widening economic inequality, dissatisfaction with employees' experiences at the workplace, along with the voices of other stakeholders demanding change, the "shareholder first" model no longer suffices. CEOs are clearly operating in a more complex environment than just a decade ago.

The overwhelming majority of American adults believe that corporations should be more than machines for maximizing shareholder value. A July 2019 survey by Fortune found that 72% of Americans agreed that public companies should be "mission driven" as well as focused on shareholders and customers. Also, 64% of Americans say that a company's "primary purpose" should include "making the world better" and they say it should include "making money for shareholders."[81]

The 2020 Edelman Trust Barometer reported that 87% say stakeholders are more important than shareholders to long-term company success. It also reported that customers and employees are over 5 times more important to a company's long-term success than shareholders.[82]

Even private equity firms and investment management companies—businesses set up to buy and make under-valued companies more valuable, and then selling them—are changing their ways. Larry Fink, CEO of BlackRock, the world's largest private equity company with seven trillion in assets under management, in his 2019 letter to portfolio-company CEOs, wrote, "Purpose is not the sole pursuit of profits but the animating force for achieving them. Profits are in no way inconsistent with purpose—in fact, profits and purpose are inextricably linked."[83]

Acknowledging these pressures, in August 2019, the Business RoundTable, an organization of CEOs of the largest US corporations, representing the companies that make up 30% of total US market capitalization, crafted a new statement on corporate purpose. This important act signals that CEOs are understanding that healthy businesses serve more than the shareholder—they must become stakeholder-centered. To thrive in the future, the needs of all stakeholders must be acknowledged and addressed. Excluding the needs of any stakeholder is a perilous path.[84] The BRT's revised statement for the purpose of the corporation is as follows:

Americans deserve an economy that allows each person to succeed through hard work and creativity and to lead a life of meaning and dignity. We believe the free-market system is the best means of generating good jobs, a strong and sustainable economy, innovation, a healthy environment, and economic opportunity for all.

Business plays a vital role in the economy by creating jobs, fostering innovation, and providing essential goods and services. Businesses make and sell consumer products; manufacture equipment and vehicles; support the national defense; grow and produce food; provide health care; generate and deliver energy, and offer financial, communications, and other services that underpin economic growth.

While each of our individual companies serves its own corporate purpose, we share a fundamental commitment to all of our stakeholders. We commit to:

Delivering Value to Our Customers. We will further the tradition of American companies leading the way in meeting or exceeding customer expectations.

Investing in Our Employees. This starts with compensating them fairly and providing important benefits. It also includes supporting them through training and education that help develop new skills for a rapidly changing world. We foster diversity and inclusion, dignity, and respect.

Dealing Fairly and Ethically with Our Suppliers. We are dedicated to serving as good partners to other companies, large and small, that help us meet our missions.

Supporting the Communities in Which We Work. We respect the people in our communities and protect the environment by embracing sustainable practices across our businesses.

Generating Long-Term Value for Shareholders. They provide the capital that allows companies to invest, grow, and innovate. We are committed to transparency and effective engagement with shareholders.

Each of our stakeholders is essential. We commit to deliver value to all of them, for the future success of our companies, our communities, and our country.

The revised purpose statement from the Business RoundTable is an encouraging start.

Research shows that companies with high levels of purpose outperform the market by 5-7% per year, on par with companies with best-in-class governance and innovative capabilities. They also grow faster and have higher profitability. The link between purpose and profitability is present only if senior leadership has been successful in diffusing that sense of purpose further down in the organization, especially in middle management, and in providing clarity on how to achieve that purpose.

The CEO's job is to make the company more valuable—in a sustainable way—that benefits all stakeholders. Even in a historic bull market, most CEOs aren't creating the value and impact they could or should.

Value isn't just increasing the market capitalization of the firm. It's also about increasing the value of human capital. It's about increasing the value in the relationships with customers, the community, and suppliers. It's about improving the capabilities of the company to compete in the future. The CEO has to be Chief Value Creator, but that's a role few CEOs have seized and mastered. A good way to create greater value is for CEOs to focus on operating in a more purpose-driven way, which builds clarity, trust, and confidence.

Today, CEOs should recognize they likely have a collective purpose problem and a trust problem within their companies. Consider the latest findings. The 2019 Human Capital Trends study by Deloitte[85] found that:

- When asked about their trust in leadership, only 46% rated their organization as effective or very effective;
- Only 53% felt their organizations were effective or very effective at creating meaningful work; and
- 59% of workers were depleted in energy and lacked meaning and purpose.

Gallup's "State of The American Workplace" found that fewer than 30% of leaders operate with any sense of purpose.[86] According to the 2018 Edelman Trust Barometer, nearly 70% identified building trust as a CEO's number one job, ahead of producing high-quality products and services.[87]

In Fortune's "2019 CEO Initiative Survey," 87% agreed that the need for moral leadership in business is greater than ever. Yet only 7% of employees surveyed said their leaders often or always exhibited the behaviors of moral leadership.[88]

CEOs have collective work to do to flip these perceptions. It's time to reinvent the CEO's role to one that creates more value for all stakeholders. Are you operating like the Chief Value Officer? As the CEO, you are either creating value or destroying value. Are you winning or losing? Which is it?

Here's a recommended list of actions CEOs can take to lead with purpose and create value for all:

1. CEOs should identify and articulate a collective purpose for their enterprise and a set of values that they can live according to with integrity. Purpose is like fuel. The research shows that companies that define, communicate, and operate on purpose perform at a higher level.

2. CEOs should examine how they operate in their role today and reinvent as necessary. They should dig for, write, and communicate their own authentic purpose. They should show how their individual purpose is connected to the company's purpose. Leading with purpose and passion engages hearts and minds. In this way, CEOs can have a more powerful impact. As purpose is shared, authenticity is shown, trust increases, and the CEO stands on a more credible platform to operate as chief value creator for their enterprise to lead change and growth.

3. CEOs should envision and build a leadership team and workforce that is purpose-driven and creates great impact. Imagine if all leaders and team members created great value and impact. What has to happen for that to occur? A company of reinvented leaders is

the force multiplier for creating value and impact across the company.

4. Turn leaders and mid-managers into purpose-driven, passionate, productive, and reinvented leaders who create value and impact. Connect all in the workforce to the collective company purpose. As CEOs raise their individual games and become role models for others, they should invite, encourage, and support other leaders in the company to do the same with their team members. Support them in creating their own purpose statements. Train them to communicate their personal purpose with their teams and to discuss how it links to the company's reason for being and their own professional lives. Help front-line team members see how the collective purpose connects to their roles and day-to-day tasks. Invite their followers to create individual purpose statements —like the KPMG team members did—to get purpose-focused. Show leaders how to coach value into existence. Hold leaders accountable to do so.

CEOs who adopt these steps will be on the path to creating great value and impact. They understand their mandate has gone beyond shareholders to stakeholders to ensure their firm thrives by doing well and doing good.

"When I went to business school, they said, 'Focus on your shareholder, Marc. The business of business is business.' That no longer applies. We have to erase that from our history books. The business of business is improving the state of the world."
Marc Benioff, Chairman and CEO, Salesforce.com

Appendix 2: Leaders Are the Force Multiplier for Impact

As a leader, it's your job to get results, to create value and impact in a sustainable way. Your job is to inspire your followers by your example. To get everyone aligned. To help each person become their best. Do these things and you are a value creator. You create great impact. Fail to do these things and you are a value destroyer.

As a leader, are you performing like this? Are you a value creator or a value destroyer?

Consider these statistics about the state of leadership today:

- Fewer than 20% of leaders have a strong sense of their own individual purpose.[89]
- Only 49% agreed they get to use their strengths to do what they do best every day.[90]
- 58% of workers trust strangers more than their own boss.[91]
- 60% of workers have left a job or would leave a job over a bad boss.[92]
- 65% of workers say they'd take a new boss over a pay raise.[93]
- 70% of employees are disengaged at work.[94]
- 75% say their bad boss is the worst part of their workplace.[95]
- 79% don't feel appreciated by the boss.[96]
- 83% of US workers suffer from work-related stress. The main source of stress at work is their boss.[97]

These are damning findings about the state of leadership. These shared perceptions point to a leadership crisis. If you are a leader, the odds are you've got a problem. Flip these statements around and try them on yourself? What would your people say about you?

To compound the leadership effectiveness problem, there is a leadership shortage. With baby boomers retiring and leaving the workforce, companies are worried about the readiness of other leaders to succeed the departing ones.

In the 2019 Global Human Capital Trends report, Deloitte reported: "Eighty percent of executives rate leadership as a high priority for their organizations. But only forty-one percent think their organizations are ready to meet their leadership requirements."[98] A leadership crisis combined with a leadership shortage is a disaster. But it is also an opportunity for you, if you are committed to becoming the best leader you can be and creating great impact.

How's your self-awareness? Most leaders are unaware of how they impact others. Seventy-five percent of leaders think they are in the top ten percent of leadership. That's statistically impossible. The bottom fifty percent of the class at Harvard Medical School couldn't be in the top ten percent of their profession either. For leaders, this means sixty-five percent are delusional. When was the last time you completed a 360-degree feedback assessment of yourself?

You may have been a leader for many years. You may be smart with a high IQ. You may have considerable expertise and experience in your industry. You may have an MBA from a top-tier school. You may point to your track record of promotions and results and believe you've been successful. Perhaps. Those are the hallmarks of twentieth century success. What made you successful in the past is no assurance you'll be successful in the future, if you don't reinvent. The rules for leading have changed.

Would your followers say you don't have a sense of your individual purpose? Do your team members trust strangers more than you? Do they feel unappreciated? Are they disengaged? Do they suffer from stress you have induced?

If you answered "yes' to any of the questions above, you are failing as a leader. Any question that you have answered "yes" is due to the way people are treated by you and the environment you create.

Where do you stand?

As the leader, you've been given a gift. The gift of leadership is a privilege. When you lead others, and do it well, it is the most noble of professions. It's a responsibility and an opportunity. There is no other occupation where you can help so many others learn and grow. It provides you, as the leader, the opportunity and the responsibility for making an indelible contribution to the lives of your followers. As a bonus, you get to be recognized for your team's achievements and impact when you succeed.

To thrive and flourish in these times, in today's hypercompetitive, volatile and uncertain world, where virtually every company is reinventing its business model and the way it operates due to technological disruptions, relentless competition, shifting demographics, and generational preferences, you have to reinvent yourself. Unfortunately, few leaders are reinventing themselves. If you aren't reinventing yourself, learning and growing continuously, you've got a problem. Your career, your earnings, your dreams— they are all at risk.

"Save yourself, and you will save a thousand around you."
Saint Seraphim of Sarov

To reinvent as a leader is to consciously transform how you operate, connect, and lead so you can stay relevant and energized, capable of creating maximum value.

The question is, how do you do this?

You start by serving your people extraordinarily well. To help them be successful at work and in their lives.

Here are the new rules of leadership:

1. Your #1 Role is to Lead by Example

You dictate all behavior, not by your orders or mandates, but by your example.

Why is this so important? Because people learn by mimicking. It's a "monkey see, monkey do" world. As the leader, everyone is always looking at you. You are always on stage. People don't go as fast as they can. They only go as fast you, the leader. Your speed determines the speed of your pack. That is why you have to be excellent in everything you do.

As the leader, you have to be the most positive, the most purposeful, the most passionate, the most productive, and the most impactful. You need to be the most disciplined, the most consistent, the most authentic, the most service-driven, the most committed to learning, the most committed to growth, and the most committed to reinvention.

Think about Usain Bolt, who won the gold medal and set the world record in the 100 meters in the 2012 London Olympics. He ran the 100 meters in only 9.63 seconds. Not only did Bolt set the record, but the silver and bronze medalists both finished the race under 9.8 seconds, the first time in history for the top three finishers. When Yohan Blake and Justin Gatlin, the silver and bronze medalists, were asked how they ran so fast, they answered, "Trying to catch Usain." Bolt didn't just win the 100 meters in 2012. He won gold in the 100 meters and 200 meters in 2008, 2012 and 2016. He is the only sprinter in history to have ever done so.[99]

The speed of Usain Bolt—the leader—determined the speed of the pack. He set the pace, the standard, for the competition. He raised everyone's games. His competitors ran faster because of him. As the leader of your group, you have to do the same.

Do you hold yourself to the highest standard, like Usain Bolt did in the sprints? Do you expect excellence of yourself? You must hold yourself to the highest standard first before you can hold your team members accountable for excellence.

When you fly on a plane, the flight attendant in her pre-flight instructions reminds you that in case of an emergency, you must put the oxygen mask on your face first before helping others. The same is true for creating impact. You'll need to gain clarity of your purpose, gifts, strengths, and passions first. You will need to recraft your role and turbocharge your productivity first so that you can create great value and impact. Then, show and coach others so they discover and excel, too.

People want to commit to a purpose, to people, profit, and the planet. People want to be inspired. Leaders who operate with purpose, passion, and productivity are a company's force multiplier. They are the untapped source of value for most companies because only a few leaders are operating to create value and impact. Most are managing for output and maybe engagement.

Are you leading like the leader you would want to follow? Where do you need to improve, learn, grow, and reinvent? What commitments have you made to become your best and create great impact?

2. Reinvent Yourself
To reinvent yourself as a leader, start by creating and articulating your individual purpose, your values and then living them with integrity.

Show your people how to connect their purpose with the collective purpose of your business. They likely don't know their gifts (what others perceive) and talents. They may not know what they're blessed with. Help them discover their purpose, gifts, and talents. They've likely lost touch with their passions. How about helping them find their passions?

Leaders with purpose who communicate this purpose to their followers inspire their people to be[100]:

- 2.8 times more likely to stay at the company;

- 2.2 times more likely to have higher job satisfaction; and
- 70% more satisfied with their jobs.

Virtually everyone wants purpose and meaning in their work and life.

DeVry U Career Advisory Board studied millennials' attitudes regarding their work. They found that seventy-one percent of millennials ranked finding meaningful work as one of the top three key elements they used to evaluate their success. Thirty percent reported it as the single most important element. It was also reported that they were willing to sacrifice more traditional career comforts in pursuit of more meaningful work.[101]

Once people have a sense of their individual purpose, how about helping them express their purpose through their work and showing them how to identify and apply their passions and energy? As purpose is defined and they get more passionate about their work, how about showing them how to be more productive using the OKR productivity system to get more done with less effort? So they can create greater value.

People who aren't purposeful, passionate, and productive simply don't increase their value or their company's value.

Need more proof? Deloitte Insights reported that "purpose-driven" companies tend to have thirty percent higher productivity and forty percent higher levels of retention.

3. Get Everyone Aligned
The leader makes the difference between success and failure as to whether the team, company, or country succeeds or fails. As the leader, you are the one who can draw out extraordinary efforts of people or you can be the cause of your team's downfall. High performance is only made possible through alignment—it's your job. A talented team of people that lacks alignment and focus loses.

As work becomes increasingly digitized and information is ubiquitous, the role of managers and leaders as coordinators of work has largely disappeared. The challenge now is creating alignment as you are leading virtual teams, working under flexible arrangements, managing multi-generational and diverse groups, and supporting the flow of knowledge.

How do you align? You get alignment by everyone understanding the vision, purpose, and values of the company. Everyone must understand how their role contributes to the greater purpose of the company. Get everyone on the same page about the Objectives and Key Results to be achieved, and also how their OKRs support the company. Communicate how decisions are made and who has decision rights. Help your team members understand the impact their contributions have on the company. This will foster a feeling of purpose, belonging, and connectedness. Practice transparency. That's what alignment is all about.

Few employees are adding the value they are capable of creating. It's your job to help them contribute more, to add more value, and to become better versions of themselves.

4. Help People Become Their Best
When you encourage your people to define and communicate their purposes, ignite their passions, and turbocharge their productivity, you are on your way. Help them grow professionally and personally. Understand and help them achieve their dreams.

Matthew Kelly, author of *The Dream Manager*, writes, "If you want employees to contribute heart and mind to the enterprise, then you must commit heart and mind to helping them achieve their dreams—to develop as persons who not only serve today's customer with verve but are in a position to move on and move forward in the crazy-getting-crazier world in which they are imbedded."[102]

"The key to creating an ownership culture is getting to people's hearts. You have to get to people's pride."
Joe Kaeser, CEO, Siemens

Tom Peters writes in his brilliant book, *The Excellence Dividend: Meeting the Tech Tide with Work that Works and Jobs that Last*, about the importance of a leader helping others become their best versions of themselves. He shares his *Corporate Mandate 2018*: "Your principal moral obligation as a leader is to develop the skill set of every one of the people in your charge (temporary as well as semi-permanent) to the maximum extent of your abilities and in ways that are consistent with their 'revolutionary' needs in the years ahead. The bonus: This is also the #1 profit maximization strategy!"[103]

Is that your principal moral obligation as a leader?

Here are two questions for you to consider:

Does everyone who works under you grow as people?

While working under you, do they become better, wiser, more purposeful, passionate, more energetic, more productive, and better able to create greater impact?

A powerful way to connect with and coach your followers is to implement a regular meeting to build individual responsibility, the W-5 (Work in 5 directions) meeting. A W-5 session offers a powerful opportunity to promote self-accountability and professional development. The five directions of work are: customer, direct reports, peers, manager, and self-development.

When you hold these sessions every week – or at least – every other week, in the right spirit, you'll hold your team members accountable only when they don't hold themselves accountable. The goals of these meetings are to develop your team members, help them learn and grow, commit to constant improvement and commit to achieving maximum impact.[104]

The purpose of this forty-five minute meeting is to discuss the team member's OKR performance, and how she's growing and learning. It is the team member's responsibility to schedule and lead the meeting. She explains how she is meeting and exceeding the requirements in each of the five directions, and a plan to correct any deficiencies. She brings up specific co-workers with whom she frequently interacts, the quality of the interaction, and the strength of the working relationship. She covers successes and failures, shortcomings and accomplishments.

The two of you identify specific areas in which you can assist. The spirit is open and non-judgmental, and the coaching is honest and collaborative. Look for ways to encourage, support, and recognize her. After the team member nears the end of the discussion with you, ask how you can help her achieve results—support her. Ask questions such as the following:

- What are you working on? How are your OKRs coming along?
- What's getting in your way?
- What are the roadblocks you face?
- How can I best help you be more successful?
- How are you growing and developing to achieve your career goals?

"Three things every human being wants most: to be seen, heard, and understood."
Oprah Winfrey

Think team members don't want W-5 sessions? According to PwC, 60% of employees—and 72% of millennial employees—desire feedback daily or weekly. A study conducted by Adobe showed that 80% of office workers want immediate, in-the-moment feedback.[105]

A Workhuman 2019 global employee survey, "The Future of Work is Human," revealed that team members who check in with their manager at least weekly are more than twice as likely to trust their manager.[106] W-5s are the linchpin of continuous performance management, the leader's moment for rich conversation, feedback, and recognition.

In addition to promoting self-accountability and strengthening alignment, the W-5 meeting gives you as a leader, a power platform for recognizing and energizing your people. Perhaps no human need is more neglected in the workplace than feeling valued. The need for significance in work is a manifestation of our inborn hunger for meaning in our lives. People have a genuine hunger to be recognized, respected, and genuinely cared about. That's your job, leader. As they operate by purpose and perform, remember what people really want. To feel good and validated. There are two things people can't give themselves: personal attention and appreciation. The number one reason companies lose top talent is that they didn't feel appreciated.

"The only thing more powerful than sex and money is praise and recognition."
Mary Kay Ash

As the leader, are your recognizing and appreciating your people sufficiently?

Twenty-five percent? Or one hundred percent? Think about each of your team members. Most of them can probably "meet expectations" with two hands tied behind their back. They can easily perform ordinary, satisfactory work. That takes maybe 25% of their effort.

What about the other 75%? Are you getting the other 75% of their capability, too?

Getting the other 75% is voluntary and is entirely based on you. It's based on how well you inspire them. How do you get the other 75%? Give them a challenge. Invite them to operate with purpose to create a great impact and to tackle huge dreams. Coach, praise and recognize them.

Whose List Will You Be On?

One last thought, when the people who have worked under you put their list of "Best Bosses" together, who's list will you be on? What is your legacy in the collective minds of your followers – both current and past? Is that legacy what you'd like it to be? Would they say you are among the best leaders they ever worked for? Did you help them learn, grow, and become their best as people? Did you help them live better lives? Did you touch their lives indelibly?

Reinvent yourself, leader. Lead by example. Get all aligned. Help others become the best versions of themselves. Do this and you'll be a massive value creator. You'll create great impact.

Appendix 3: Encourage Purpose in Your Children

Forty years ago, after graduating high school, you either went to work at the factory, joined the military, enrolled in vocational school to learn a trade, or entered college. The options were pretty straight forward and there was an implicit "deal" of what you could expect from each choice. Graduates made their decision and could more or less follow their paths to a middle-class life.

Today, young people have limitless options. That is both exciting and terrifying. What's missing is they've got no clear answers. As young people think a lot about their futures, this lack of clarity too often creates anxiety and depression. They see a volatile and uncertain world that feels scary and threatening.

For far too many youngsters, the stress is too much to handle. The National Institutes of Health reports one in three of all adolescents ages 13 to 18 will experience an anxiety disorder. Other studies show a sharp rise in depression among teens and young adults over the last decade.[107]

While there are a number of reasons that drive the increase in anxiety and depression of young people, worry about the future contributes to their decline in mental well-being.

If ever there was a time for parents to get connected with their kids and help them, it's now. This is where parents need to step in. An excellent source for parents and caring adults is William Damon's book, *The Path to Purpose: How Young People Find Their Calling in Life.* Damon is a Stanford University professor on adolescence.[108]

Damon writes, "In our interviews and surveys, only about one in five young people in the 12-26-year age range express a clear vision of where they want to go, what they want to accomplish in life, and why. The largest portion of those we interviewed – almost 60% – may have engaged in some potentially purposeful activities, or they may have developed some vague aspirations; but they do not have any real commitment to such activities or any realistic plans for pursuing their aspirations. The remaining portion of today's youth population – almost a quarter of those we interviewed – express no aspirations *at all*. In some cases, they claim that they see no point in acquiring any."

He describes four groups of young people.

The Disengaged express no interest in purpose, and they made up 20% of the sample of twelve hundred young people between 12 and 26.

The Dreamers consisted of 25% of the sample. Dreamers had ideas about purposes but had done little or nothing to actively try out their ideas.

The Dabblers were those who had engaged in some activities that were potentially purposeful but showed few signs of committing themselves to these pursuits over time. Dabblers represented 31% of the sample.

Finally, those who found something meaningful to dedicate themselves to, sustained this interest over a period of time, and expressed a clear sense of what they were trying to accomplish and why, made up 20% of the group. He described this group as the Purposeful.

If you have young people in the world you care about, which group do you believe they fall into today?

As a parent or caring adult, there is an opportunity you have to assist your children discover their purpose.

The hectic lifestyles of many parents spill into the lives of children. With everyone on the go, family interactions fray and face-to-face connections decrease. When parents do try to help their kids, their suggestions are usually tactical in nature, offering no strategy. Statements like, "Get good grades," don't provide useful direction or clarity to the "Why?" and "What kind of work will I do when I get older?"

Damon believes that if young people had a goal in mind and then went to college or other post-high school training with that purpose in mind, taking classes to prepare themselves for achieving it, saying, "Here's what I need to do in order to fulfill my dream," that would be a much superior approach than simply saying, "Get the degree and figure out why later."

When young people have a destination, the right decisions along their journey become clearer. Without purpose, being a good kid can feel like an arbitrary list of things to do and not do. With purpose, doing the right thing is clear because it's in service of a greater goal.

Damon writes, ""Once a young person has taken on a purposeful quest, his or her personality begins to be transformed by the activities and events of the quest. Out of necessity, the youngster acquires such capacities as resourcefulness, persistence, know-how, and a tolerance of risk and temporary setback. Character virtues such as diligence, responsibility, confidence, and humility get a boost from the experience of making a commitment to a challenging purpose and seeing it through. What's more, literacies of all kinds (verbal, mathematical, cultural) develop in ways that extend well beyond anything previously learned in the youngster's home or classroom."

What can you do to help young people discover their purpose?

Start by being a good role model. When you convey your individual purpose and your values, and how you chose those, that's a great start. Share the meaning you get from your work. Your job does more than pay the bills. What is it that you do that makes the world a better place, contributes to the common good, or makes someone happy?

For instance, how did you know you wanted to raise a family? At what point did you know you wanted to be a marketing manager, a police officer, a principal, a _____? Share the meaningful experiences from your life and your setbacks that helped you gain this insight. Whatever your purpose is, discuss how you knew it was your calling and how it contributes to your everyday life satisfaction. When your children see you living a life of purpose, impact, and joy, they'll be encouraged to do the same.

If you regret not following your dreams, don't shy away from relaying those lessons learned to your children. This may help them gain knowledge from your experience.

Share with your children that what they do matters. While they get told what to do a lot at school and home, this will change over time. They have the personal power to make decisions and take actions. They will be able to make decisions and will be called on to make a difference. They can make the world a better place. If they don't make a difference somewhere to someone, life isn't going to feel very meaningful. The choices they make and the actions they take matter. People cannot have a sense of purpose until they know how much they matter. When young people have the confidence to know they matter, they can begin to imagine their purpose in life.

Realize you aren't the creator of your child's purpose. You don't create purpose and passion for your kids any more than you can create their personality. What you can do is to gently ask questions about their opinions and interests. You can expose them to new things and see how they respond. You can introduce options. You can encourage them to go deeper to experience and learn more about topics that resonate. Pay attention to what drives them to keep learning. If a teen loves writing stories, and is challenged to write more to improve, encourage that passion. Their talent and interest could help them find a life of purpose that is right for them. Create a safe environment for dialogue. Dinners, watching the news together, and trips in the car each offer organic situations that lend themselves to discussing topics that are important to your youngster. You can ask them why their topics of interest fascinate them. It's better to have small, frequent conversations, too. This is a process, not a one and done discussion.

Avoid questions like "What do you want to do with your life?" Instead, ask non-intimidating questions such as, "When was a time you helped someone?" or "What do you think your best qualities are?" "What kinds of things do you really care about and why?" "What does it mean to have a good life?" "What does it mean to be a good person?"

Let your kids know they have unique gifts. Describe the gifts you see them possessing and have a dialogue with them to get them to hear their perceptions of their gifts. Explore ideas with them about how they might use their gifts at school, in extracurricular activities, at volunteering opportunities, and in the future.

Identify and discuss examples of purposeful young people. Sometimes it is useful to have an example or two of young people who have discovered their purpose. While everyone has their own path to discovering purpose, Damon's book has several examples of young people who have followed their purposes and have made a difference. The story of Ryan Hreljac, was particularly inspiring.

Ryan learned at age 6 in school that many people in Africa had a hard time getting access to clean water. Ryan began doing chores to raise money to build a well, which led to other fund-raising activities. Within twelve months, he had raised $2,000, which was the cost to build a well. He sent the money to Water Can, and a well was drilled in northern Uganda, alongside a public school. Two years went by and he raised $61,000 to build wells. His story was picked up on The Oprah Winfrey Show.

His parents helped him set up a registered charity, Ryan's Well Foundation, to educate school children about water issues and to get more people involved in fundraising and well digging. A number of years later, the foundation brought clean water to nearly 900,000 people in sixteen developing countries through nearly 1200 water and sanitation projects.

Not everyone will create a purpose like Ryan's Well Foundation, which has such a far-reaching impact. Yet everyone can have a purpose that has an impact in the world, even in small ways. Educating and inspiring your child with stories like Ryan's can be the spark that lights the flame.

Encourage volunteer work. Volunteer work is a wonderful way to finding something meaningful. When teens experience the personal satisfaction from doing something that makes a difference in the world, they develop their personal beliefs and values, which leads to healthy development and a sense of purpose. Resources such as DoSomething.org can connect teens to volunteer opportunities.

Introduce your children to trusted adults who can be mentors. If they express an interest in a profession or field, think of who you can introduce them to who has some experience in their area of interest. Maybe you can't describe what it is like to be a trial lawyer – but your cousin, the trial lawyer can. Your doctor can speak to the process of preparing for and getting accepted to medical school and the path to becoming a physician, if that is an area of interest. Connecting them with trusted mentors outside the home is very powerful. Damon identified twelve youngsters who were highly purposeful in his book. Every one of them had a mentor outside the home.

Help them develop an entrepreneur's mindset. Encourage an entrepreneurial attitude by supporting them in stepping outside their comfort zone into the world around them. Maybe it is an after-school club or activity, a part-time job, or exploring the local community with friends. Maybe it is to fundraise for a special cause, to sign up for a camp, or to study abroad. You never know what might stick. Think about taking a mindset that is about "offense" and not "defense." It's about developing a growth mindset with empowering beliefs. Encourage your child to take on challenges and healthy risks when trying new activities.

Damon writes, "Cultivating an entrepreneurial spirt means encouraging the following attitudes: 1. The ability to set goals and make realistic plans to accomplish them; 2. An optimistic, can-do attitude; 3. Persistence in the face of obstacles and difficulties; 4. A tolerance – or more, even an appetitive – for risk; 5. Resilience in the face of failure; 6. Determination to achieve measurable results; and 7. Resourcefulness and inventiveness in devising the means to achieve those results."

Show optimism. Stay optimistic about their future while helping them be resilient. They will experience adversity along their journey. Their beliefs about adversity are what drives the consequences of the adversity. There is always a better way to look at a setback than as a failure. Setbacks are the lessons to get you closer to your purpose and desired destination. That's a mindset of optimism and resilience.

Be patient. Discovering purpose is not a single event – it's a process. Young people will go at their own pace. Remind them that life is an ongoing process of change. It's OK not to have an answer right away on purpose, as it takes experience and time. Remind your youngsters that you are there to support them and love them no matter what.

While you can provide guidance on different routes to travel, and you can introduce options and allow exploration within safe limits, they'll sort through choices to determine what is best for them. With your support and interest, they'll discover their purpose in time. This process of encouraging purpose will put them on a path to creating a life of impact.

Appendix 4: Do Well By Doing Good!

By Jack Morgan

Remember our friend Jack Morgan? His story opened this book. In this chapter, Jack tells us in his own words how he uncovered his purpose and created an impact story and plan.

When we got together to discuss where I was, Chuck gave me a number of questions on which to reflect. The questions helped me gain clarity about what was really important. It wasn't just the questions that helped. Thinking through it all helped me see what I truly wanted, so I could put together a plan to make some necessary changes.

What I quickly realized was that I was way too comfortable. I'd gotten soft. I wasn't focused on meaning or purpose. While I was working long hours and I was away from home a lot, I wasn't working as smart as I could have been. I wasn't creating the value I could have created. I was too often working on issues that my direct reports should have been tackling. I wasn't always showing up like a pro, I realized. As I look back, I was going through the motions at times, definitely not deliberately learning, growing, and reinventing.

When Chuck asked me to describe who I was, what I was doing, and who I was called to be, I remember answering, "Medical device company president, growing the company for the shareholders, CEO, board, customers, and our team members." That was the wrong order.

This process helped me zero in and get clear about my purpose. Reflecting back to when I was a teen, I remembered what spurred my interest in healthcare and ultimately the medical technology sector. I started in sales and became a sales leader and an executive.

My dad's older brother, Uncle Dick, worked as a carpenter, and his wife, my Aunt Debbie, was a secretary. Uncle Dick loved his family and worked hard to support them. When I was in high school, Uncle Dick was diagnosed with pancreatic cancer and died within a year. It was an awful time, and I saw my aunt and three cousins suffer. Uncle Dick didn't have good healthcare insurance. His family not only lost their husband and dad, but they lost their primary provider of income. They got sacked with the bills. They lost their home. They lived with us for a nearly a year. It was horrible what they went through. What happened to my aunt and cousins, after the tragedy of losing Uncle Dick, struck me as being unfair and unjust. It left an impression on me that it wasn't right that someone who died of an awful disease should have their family suffer like that and lose all their assets.

When it was time for college, I wasn't an engineering or science kind of guy. I liked business, sales, and the idea of competing against other companies. So, I chose marketing as my major. During my senior year, when it was time to interview for jobs, I interviewed with healthcare and pharmaceutical companies, and I got a job as a sales representative for a company that sold disposable products for hospital operating rooms. That's how my career started, carrying the sales bag. The idea of working for a company that improves the quality of people's lives grabbed me.

Thirty plus years, several promotions, and two other companies later, there I was. My focus had slowly drifted from improving lives to growing the business for the sake of growth. I had taken for granted the "improving people's lives" part.

Doing the impact work and my reflection, that gave me ideas and then a plan that changed everything. I know where I'm going and why. Let me tell you the story.

Here's what happened. Kiki and I had a heart to heart about what was most important to us. We talked about the importance of our faith, our marriage, our family, and where we wanted to see ourselves in ten years. What is most important to us is to be purposeful, happy, and healthy, individually and as a couple. We want our kids to become well-educated, optimistic, purposeful, happy, and healthy adults.

We've been fortunate in our lives. While material things are nice, we agreed that happiness doesn't derive from the square footage of our house or the cars in our garage. We are confident that in ten years, we'll have sufficient financial resources for a comfortable retirement. So, we chose to deemphasize the material items—all the "stuff." We created a plan to simplify our lives by shedding things we didn't really need. It's been liberating!

We also agreed we each needed a purpose bigger than ourselves, our family, and work. Kiki created hers. I created mine, too. I would like to share a summary of my purpose and impact plan. Here's a summary:

- Success to me is to live a life of deep purpose, love, good health, and well-being.

- My greatest gifts are empathy coupled with a genuine desire to help others live better and healthier lives.

- My purpose statement is: *Good health should be everyone's right.*

- My inviolable values are three:
    1. Healthcare must become a universal right for all!
    2. Encourage others to live purposeful, healthy, and rewarding lives.
    3. Always leave things better than when I found them.

- To pursue my purpose with passion and vigor necessitated that I recraft my job and how my work creates value. Here's what I decided to do. I shifted my mindset from making the business plan each year to making people's lives better. I more deliberately emphasized making people's lives better through coaching and encouraging them to do great things.

To give me more time to coach, we made some structural changes within the company. I am still the president of the business and I have overall responsibility for our financial results. Without adding any new heads, we created three business units headed by general managers, each of whom report to me, and they have full profit and loss responsibility for their unit. My job is to coach them, help them become better, and identify my eventual successor.

This change allows me to focus on growing the business and coaching people.

- I chose to develop what I call a *Coaching for Growth* leadership style. I read several books on coaching. I hold bi-weekly coaching sessions with my direct reports – the work in five directions sessions or what we call "W-5s." I've included this coaching leadership style as a personal development OKR. I teach and encourage others on how to use this style, too.

  I've moved from a day-to-day focus to viewing the business longer-term. I use a more visionary leadership style. Reflecting on how I add value and what I value made what had to happen through recrafting clear.

  My vital functions are: 1. Coach and encourage others to become the best versions of themselves; 2. Align all team members to our strategy; 3. Identify breakthrough growth opportunities, such as new alliances, a digital platform, and new business models to accelerate our organization's growth.

- To turbocharge my productivity, I started saying "No!" a lot more. I committed to three vital functions. My Objectives and Key Results are refreshed quarterly. I plan my time each month, week, and day to reflect my OKRs. I use daily sprints to accelerate results.

Shortly after I made these changes and commitments, something significant happened. With new-found clarity about my purpose, I recalled a famous quote from Walter Cronkite, former anchor for CBS Evening News. He said, "America's healthcare system is neither healthy, caring, nor a system. "

I'm not sure when Cronkite made that comment. Since he's been dead for over a decade it has to be at least ten years. While it was true then, it is even more true today. Our healthcare system is broken and is becoming more broken as the Affordable Care Act has been attacked the past three years. It is harder for the vulnerable to get Medicaid coverage. We need a universal healthcare system so everyone is covered in this country, along the lines of Medicare for all.

As a country, our healthcare costs are double those of other industrialized countries, while we have lower life expectancy, higher infant-mortality rates, and worse outcomes than other advanced nations. We need to do better as a country.

This healthcare problem gets my fires burning. My passion is to use my role to support and pursue good healthcare for all Americans — not just people like me who are blessed to have excellent health insurance provided by their employers. I don't believe the answer is having a one-payor system. I believe people who like their healthcare coverage should be allowed to continue it. However, in our country, which is the world's richest, we've got to get everyone who isn't covered under a universal healthcare umbrella. It's appalling to me that life expectancy in the US has been on the decline since 2016. Did you know that if you live in Mississippi, your life expectancy is less than the life expectancy of people in Mexico?

Additionally, people who get sick shouldn't go broke. Five hundred thousand people in the US go bankrupt each year due to medical costs – just like my Uncle Dick's family did. That's not right and it has to be changed.

Until we have universal health coverage, we will need to do the best we can to bring healthcare to those most in need—somehow, some way. Something has got to be done, and there are things I can do, things I'm doing, in a small way to help this cause.

Recrafting my role has given me more capacity to pursue my purpose: *Good health should be everyone's right.*

Following an introduction from a physician friend of mine, I've volunteered and now sit on the board of a non-profit whose goal is to provide healthcare to those most needy in rural America. Remote Area Medical is a non-profit provider of mobile medical clinics delivering free dental, vision, and medical care to underserved and uninsured individuals. It was originally created to treat people in the developing world but turned its attention to those in need of healthcare across the US.

We plan and put on what are essentially large pop-up free clinics all across the country. We use old school buildings or factories. RAM relies on donations and on volunteers from companies and communities, as well as physicians, dentists, optometrists, and nurses.

There are over fifty million rural Americans who live in healthcare shortage areas where the number of hospitals, family doctors, surgeons, and paramedics has declined.[109] There are so many who have slipped through the cracks. If ACA is destroyed, millions more will lose their health coverage. Shame on us as a nation. This is an embarrassment to our country.

We see people who come to these fairs with anxiety, depression, digestive disorders, heart murmurs, high blood pressure, precancerous tumors, open wounds, unmanaged heart conditions, COPD, Type-2 diabetes. You name it, they have it.

The obesity, opioid, and unemployment problems in rural America add fuel to this epidemic. People will drive hundreds of miles and camp out for two or three days to secure their place in line for diagnosis, treatment, and some relief. For some, RAM is their last hope. So, this is an urgent and real need.

As an experienced leader in the medical device industry, my volunteer work with RAM is heading the corporate development efforts. I get to tell the story of RAM, of the need to provide healthcare to these fifty million Americans. I have the opportunity to persuade my connections and others to join and support our efforts, to donate supplies, dollars, and people. Over the years, I've met a lot of doctors. So, I reach out to them, too, as we're always in need of docs, nurses, dentists, and other professionals to staff our health fairs.

I'm also working with our industry's professional organizations, like Medical Alley in Minnesota and the international Advamed, to create understanding of the need for universal healthcare, to invite them to join our efforts, and to lobby US lawmakers for change. It's a moral and societal problem that affects thirteen percent of the US population – that's nearly forty-three million people. They have no health insurance. Many of these people are in dire need of healthcare, so in addition to heath care for all being a moral imperative, in my view, it is also good business. If all of these uninsured people had coverage, the pie gets bigger. That's good for the companies, hospitals, insurance companies, GPOs (group purchasing organizations), and IDNs (integrated delivery networks) that serve the healthcare needs of Americans. It's a way of <u>doing well by doing good</u>.

Kiki has renewed her nursing certification and now she serves patients quarterly at the RAM health fair on weekends, too. It's hard work, but it's incredibly fulfilling. It's a wonderful cause to serve together. This volunteer work breaks our hearts, but to serve these people also sets ours hearts on fire. I feel passionate again. I'm making an impact.

My commitment to creating greater impact has led me to make some different lifestyle changes. Too many years of traveling and eating too much has led me to learn I can't get away with the decisions I made in the past. I've committed to becoming healthier. In eighteen months, I've dropped twenty-five pounds, I'm exercising five times a week, and my energy has surged.

I've created three OKRs for how I'll create impact. They are as follows:

Recraft My Role To Create More Value:
- Spend 80% of work time on my vital functions: 1. Coach and encourage others to become the best versions of themselves; 2. Align all on our strategy; 3. Identify breakthrough growth opportunities and capitalize on them (including new alliances and business models to accelerate our organization's growth).
- Conduct W-5 sessions with each of my direct reports – bi-weekly.
- Sponsor executive team to discover their purpose and complete their individual impact work, in preparation for *Everyone's Got a Purpose* initiative. End of Q1.
- With the exec team, actively support, encourage, and fund *Everyone's Got a Purpose* initiative to offer all of our company's team members as a means to discover their individual purposes by year-end. MBWA (manage by wandering around) for impromptu one-on-ones with team members to hear their purposes and discuss *Everyone's Got a Purpose* progress – two hours per week.

Operate on Purpose: "Good Health Should Be Everyone's Right!"
- Actively participate in RAM board meetings each quarter.
- Drive RAM corporate development efforts – ongoing.

- Volunteer at one RAM health fair weekend per quarter.
- Speak at professional association conferences and with lawmakers about RAM with an invitation to support – quarterly.
- Direct outreach to two or more physicians or clinicians per month to tell the RAM story and invite them to learn more.
- Outreach to two or more industry executives per month to tell the RAM story and request support.

Create More Personal Impact!
- Continue to lobby elected leaders, professional associations, and industry CEOs for universal healthcare and rural access to good healthcare – *Do Well by Doing Good* initiative – ongoing.
- Continue healthy lifestyle; Keto diet; exercise – ongoing.
- Continue to simplify life – ongoing.
- Continue to serve RAM together with Kiki – quarterly.
- Continue to encourage our children to define purpose and live lives of impact - ongoing.

When Chuck first asked me who I was, what I was doing, and who I was called to do it for, I remember answering, "Medical device company president, growing a company, for the shareholders, CEO, board, customers, and our team members." This has all changed.

Now, I lead my company purposefully so it grows and makes a big impact for all its stakeholders, starting with our team members, then customers, and then investors.

I support and serve RAM's mission to bring free medical, dental, and vision care to underserved and uninsured individuals in the rural US.

I call upon corporate and political leaders to educate and influence them to support universal and accessible healthcare to all Americans no later than the end of the decade. I'm the universal healthcare catalyst.

My Declaration: *Do Well by Doing Good! Good Health Should Be Everyone's Right!*

Appendix 5: The Game of Catch

When I was 8 years old, I was a happy 3rd grader without a care in the world, living in a small town in Kentucky with my parents, Helen and Jack Bolton.

The daughter of Swedish immigrants, Helen had wanted to be a missionary when she was young; she knew how to love and take care of people. Jack was a manager at a factory. At 6'4", 250 pounds, he was like a mountain, in my eyes: my hero.

Every day, my dad and I played a game of catch. And throwing the baseball with dad, every night, was my favorite thing. Every night, after he returned home from the plant, he heard me ask: "Daddy, daddy! Can we play catch?"

One Sunday morning in late August will forever be burned in my memory. I awoke to an empty house. A few hours later, Mom, tears streaming down her face, walked in the front door. She said she had taken dad to the emergency room. She sobbed, and uttered two haunting words: "Daddy died."

We'd played catch just the night before. Now he was gone – forever – felled by a massive heart attack. I no longer took interest in school, friends—or really, much of anything. Because the game of catch was over.

That winter, Mom took matters in her own hands. She saved the S&H Green Stamps they gave you at the Winn-Dixie supermarket when you bought groceries. One warm Saturday morning in March—early spring in Kentucky—Mom said we needed to go to Louisville to run errands. She drove us to the S&H store. She told the man behind the counter that she wanted to get the catcher's mitt that appeared on page 34 of their catalog.

More than seven months had passed since I'd last played catch. Dad and I were both left-handed, but Mom was a righty; she couldn't use his old first baseman's mitt.

Mom handed over the stamp books, and took the mitt, and we went on our way. The game of catch was about to resume.

Even though Mom wasn't that great at catch, she gave it her best. We played for three years – until I was 11. We filled the holes in our hearts that way.

Shortly before my 12th birthday, Mom and I moved to Chicago. To support us, she needed to begin working as a secretary—and to care for her parents, who were in failing health. She told me I could ride my bike to the park to play Little League baseball. There, as she had predicted, I found plenty of other boys to play catch. She retired the catcher's mitt, but by then it had served its purpose.

That game of catch with Mom was a great gift. She got me over the hump of losing Dad that way. She got me playing organized baseball, and pitching. Pitching ultimately helped pay for my college education. I was blessed to play college ball under the tutelage of outstanding coaches. I also had caring professors, and a great four years in school.

Without that game of catch with Mom, I wouldn't have…

- Gone to college.
- Enjoyed a 20-year career as a leader in the fast-growing medical device industry.
- Become a CEO coach, coached a Nobel Prize-winner, written books, or given a speech at the Harvard Business School.

Nor would I be showing leaders and teams how to reinvent themselves – so they can discover how to become their best.

Accomplishing anything of significance starts with leadership. When leaders get better, so does everyone around them. Great leaders inspire others to become their best, to do extraordinary things.

Mom was a great leader. She was the person who was most generous and inspiring, who taught me to care for others. From her, I learned how to treat people, how to handle life's curveballs, and when to swing for the fences – lessons I use daily in my work.

She also had to reinvent herself, from homemaker to single parent, breadwinner, and caregiver. She never complained; she always smiled and encouraged others. Mom was the most generous person I've ever met.

And Mom told me always to give my best—and become my best. She is my role model for reinvention and leadership. This book is for her. And for you. To help you become your best.[110]

It's time to get started.

Notes

[1] "What is Your Impact" - Oct 16, 2017 - Forbes Coaches Council - Erin Urban, https://www.forbes.com/sites/forbescoachescouncil/2017/10/16/what-is-your-impact/#f8a5d456f356.

[2] "Comfortably Numb," Pink Floyd. Source: Lyric Find. Songwriters: David Jon Gilmour / Roger Waters. BMG Rights Management, Concord Music Publishing LLC.

[3] *Americans Are Among the Most Stressed People in the World, Poll Finds,*" https://www.nytimes.com/2019/04/25/us/americans-stressful.html.

[4] Their most recent study showed a whopping 67% of people are either unengaged or disengaged at work. *Gallup State of American Workplace*, https://www.gallup.com/workplace/238085/state-american-workplace-report-2017.aspx.

[5] *Passion at work: Cultivating worker passion as a cornerstone of talent development*, Deloitte University Press. https://www2.deloitte.com/us/en/insights/topics/talent/worker-passion-employee-behavior.html.

[6] The Conference Board reports that 53% of Americans are currently unhappy at work.
Recognition is the #1 thing employees say their manager could give them to inspire them to produce great work. Global studies prove that when it comes to inspiring people to be their best at work, nothing else comes close.

[7] 61% feel the pace of technological change is moving too fast and they are no longer in control of their destiny. Edelman Trust Barometer 2020, Key Findings, Jan 27, 2020, https://www.edelman.com/trustbarometer.

[8] Ibid.

[9] James Clear blog, Thursday 3-2-1, Feb 27, 2020, jamesclear.com.

[10] *Rolling Stone Magazine*, May 9, 1974, Jon Landau.

[11] *Born to Run*, Simon & Schuster, Bruce Springsteen, 2016.

[12] "How Music Made Bruce Springsteen," The Atlantic, David Brooks, November 2016, https://www.theatlantic.com/magazine/archive/2016/11/no-surrender/501110/.

[13] *The Path To Purpose: How Young People Find Their Calling in Life*, William Damon, Free Press, 2008.

[14] Jim Conn interview by Chuck Bolton, 2019.

[15] Ra Paulette, Wikipedia, https://en.wikipedia.org/wiki/Ra_Paulette.

[16] *Cavedigger* documentary, Ra Paulette, Jeff Karoff, Journeyman Pictures, 2013.

[17] Taylor Davis Violinist, Wikipedia, https://en.wikipedia.org/wiki/Taylor_Davis_(violinist).

[18] *Good Men, Great Thoughts: A Daily Devotional*, The Brothers of SAM Group, WHPHPH Publishing, 2019, https://www.amazon.com/Good-Men-Great-Thoughts-Devotional/dp/1674018150/ref=sxts_sxwds-bia-wc1_0?cv_ct_cx=Good+Men+Great+Thoughts&keywords=Good+Men+Great+Thoughts&pd_rd_i=1674018150&pd_rd_r=1d70dcac-a607-4969-a611-b960b08cffac&pd_rd_w=vuw27&pd_rd_wg=RS5nl.

[19] Frank Pleticha interview by Chuck Bolton, 2019.

[20] Fewer than 30% of leaders operate with any sense of purpose, State of The American Workplace, Gallup https://www.gallup.com/workplace/238085/state-american-workplace-report-2017.aspx.

[21] Former KARE anchor Diana Pierce searches for "What's Next," Kevyn Burger, Minneapolis Star Tribune, May 2, 2019, http://www.startribune.com/former-kare-anchor-diana-pierce-searches-for-what-s-next/509294471/.

[22] Former KARE 11 anchor Diana Pierce relishes being in charge of "What's Next?" C.J., Minneapolis Star Tribune, October 5, 2018, http://www.startribune.com/former-kare-11-anchor-diana-pierce-relishes-being-in-charge-of-what-s-next/495314741/.

[23] *Man's Search for Meaning*, Viktor E. Frankl, 1946.

[24] *The Reinvented Leader: Five Critical Steps to Becoming Your Best*, The Reinvention Imperative Publishing, 2015, Chuck Bolton, https://www.amazon.com/Reinvented-Leader-Critical-Steps-Becoming/dp/150841078X/ref=sr_1_1?keywords=The+reinvented+leader&qid=1583341672&sr=8-1.

[25] Chris Bentley interview by Chuck Bolton, 2019.

[26] *The Reinvented Me: Five Steps to Happiness in a Crazy Busy World*, The Reinvention Imperative Publishing, 2016, Chuck Bolton, https://www.amazon.com/Reinvented-Me-Steps-Happiness-Crazy-ebook/dp/B019UDBON4.

[27] Gordon MacKenzie story from *Orbiting the Giant Hairball*, "Whisper: How to Hear the Voice of God," Multnomah, Mark Batterson, 2017.

[28] "Passion for Work is More Important than Engagement." There is a really big problem in today's workforce. Almost no one is passionate about what they do. In 2014, Deloitte released a report that found 88% of employees don't have passion for their work, and so they don't contribute their full potential. Even worse, 80% of senior managers aren't passionate about their work. Deloitte Insights, 2014, https://www2.deloitte.com/us/en/insights/topics/talent/worker-passion-employee-behavior.html.

[29] Daniel Heller story, "Whisper: How to Hear the Voice of God," Multnomah, Mark Batterson, 2017.

[30] *Drive: The Surprising Truth About What Motivates Us*, Dan Pink, Riverhead Hardcover, 2009.

[31] As Steve Jobs Once Said, "People with Passion Can Change the World," Entrepreneur, Carmine Gallo, July 8, 2015, https://www.entrepreneur.com/article/248079.

[32] Alli Swanson interview by Chuck Bolton, 2019.

[33] Via Survey of Character Strengths. https://www.viacharacter.org/www/Character-Strengths-Survey.

[34] Gallup's Clifton StrenghtsFinder, https://www.gallupstrengthscenter.com/product/en-us/10108/top-5-cliftonstrengths-access.

[35] *Frames of Mind: the Theory of Multiple Intelligences*, Basic Books, Howard Gardner, 1983.

[36] *Mindset: The New Psychology of Success*, Carol Dweck, Ballantine Books, 2007.

[37] *Barking Up the Wrong Tree: The Surprising Science Behind Why Everything You Know About Success Is (Mostly) Wrong*, Harper One, Eric Barker, 2017.

[38] "Instead of 'finding your passions' try developing it, Stanford scholars say," June 18, 2018, https://news.stanford.edu/2018/06/18/find-passion-may-bad-advice/.

[39] Bo Eason newsletter, Feb 25, 2019.

[40] Andy Mackie, *Meet the Harmonica Man*, CBS News, December 14, 2009, https://www.youtube.com/watch?v=PSpoMWQRCiU.

[41] *What Leaders Can Do Right Now to Optimize Worker Potential*, Gallup Workplace, Dan Witters and Brian Brim, October 18, 2019.

[42] "The 2019 Workforce Purpose Index," *Imperative*, 2019, https://www.2019wpi.com.

[43] "Is AI Going to be a Jobs Killer? New Reports About the Future of Work," Forbes, July 15, 2019.

[44] World Economic Forum, Jack Ma, https://www.youtube.com/watch?v=rHt-5-RyrJk.

[45] *Machine Platform Crowd: Harnessing Our Digital Future*, Andrew McAfee and Erik Brynjolfsson, WW Norton, 2017.

[46] *Humans are Underrated: What High Achievers Know that Brilliant Machines Never Will*, Penguin Random House, Geoff Colvin, 2016.

[47] *Emotional Intelligence*, Penguin Random House, Daniel Goleman, 1995.

[48] *Late Bloomers: The Power of Patience in a World Obsessed with Early Achievement*, Penguin Random House, Rich Karlgaard, 2019.

[49] "88-year old McDonald's worker serves up 'happy meals'," KARE11, Land of 10,000 Stories, Boyd Huppert, March 2019, https://www.kare11.com/article/news/local/land-of-10000-stories/88-year-old-mcdonalds-worker-serves-up-happy-meals/89-3f8d3d51-964a-4774-8914-58bfdf35ab68.

[50] "Know Your Customers' 'Jobs to be Done'." *Harvard Business Review*, Clayton Christensen, et al., September 2016, https://hbr.org/2016/09/know-your-customers-jobs-to-be-done.

[51] "'I'm Building a Cathedral!' The Role of Purpose in Motivation," *Best Practices for Business*, October 11, 2019, https://aricherlifefp.wordpress.com/2011/03/31/"i'm-building-a-cathedral"-the-role-of-purpose-in-motivation-«-best-practices-for-business/.

[52] "When Work Has Meaning, Creating a Purpose-Driven Organization," Robert Quinn & Anjan Thakor, *Harvard Business Review*, July-August 2018, https://hbr.org/2018/07/creating-a-purpose-driven-organization.

[53] "Personal Responsibility, There is No Substitute," Mike Rowe, July, 2015. https://mikerowe.com/2015/07/personalresponsibilitynosubstitute/.

[54] "What a NASA janitor can teach us about living a bigger life," *The Business Journals*, John Nemo, December 23, 2014, https://www.bizjournals.com/bizjournals/how-to/growth-strategies/2014/12/what-a-nasa-janitor-can-teach-us.html.

[55] *The Reinvented Leader: Five Critical Steps to Becoming Your Best*, The Reinvention Imperative Publishing, 2015, Chuck Bolton, https://www.amazon.com/Reinvented-Leader-Critical-Steps-Becoming/dp/150841078X/ref=sr_1_1?keywords=The+reinvented+leader&qid=1583341672&sr=8-1

[56] *So Good They Can't Ignore You*, Grand Central Publishing, Cal Newport, 2012.

[57] *Born Standing Up: A Comic's Life*, Simon & Schuster, Steve Martin, 2007.

[58] Kristin Machacek Leary interview by Chuck Bolton, 2019.

[59] "A Deceptively Simple Way to Find More Happiness at Work," New York Times, Tim Herrera, April 7, 2019, https://www.nytimes.com/2019/04/07/smarter-living/how-to-be-happier-at-work.html.

[60] "What is your life's blueprint? Martin Luther King Jr: An Extraordinary Life," *Seattle Times*, 2017, https://projects.seattletimes.com/mlk/words-blueprint.html

[61] "Reinvent Your Productivity: 7 Habits for High Performance in a Turbulent World," The Reinvention Solution Publishing, Chuck Bolton, 2018, https://www.amazon.com/Reinvent-Your-Productivity-Performance-Turbulent-ebook/dp/B07826G1SD/ref=sr_1_2?keywords=Reinvent+Your+Productivity%3A&qid=1583343840&sr=8-2.

[62] "Running on Empty" lyrics, Swallow Turn Music, Jackson Browne, 1977.

[63] *Measure What Matters: How Google, Bono and the Gates Foundation Rock the World with OKRs*, Penguin Publishing Group, John Doerr, 2018.

[64] "How much data is generated each day?" World Economic Forum, 2019, https://www.weforum.org/agenda/2019/04/how-much-data-is-generated-each-day-cf4bddf29f/.

[65] *The Reinvented Leader: Five Critical Steps to Becoming Your Best*, The Reinvention Imperative Publishing, 2015, Chuck Bolton, https://www.amazon.com/Reinvented-Leader-Critical-Steps-Becoming/dp/150841078X/ref=sr_1_1?keywords=The+reinvented+leader&qid=1583341672&sr=8-1.

[66] "Americans Check Their Phones 96 Times per Day," https://www.prnewswire.com/news-releases/americans-check-their-phones-96-times-a-day-300962643.html.

[67] "When John Doerr Brought a Gift to Google's Founders," *Wired*, April 24, 2018, https://www.wired.com/story/when-john-doerr-brought-a-gift-to-googles-founders/.

[68] *The Effective Executive: The Definitive Guide to Getting the Right Things Done*, Harper Collins Publishing, Peter Drucker, 1966.

[69] *Good to Great: Why Some Companies Make the Leap and Others Don't*, Harper Collins, Jim Collins, 2001.

[70] "'Never, ever give up:' Diana Nyad completes historic Cuba-to-Florida swim," Matt Sloane, Jason Hanna and Dana Ford, CNN, September 3, 2013,
https://www.cnn.com/2013/09/02/world/americas/diana-nyad-cuba-florida-swim/index.html.

[71] "The Unsinkable Diana Nyad: Diana Nyad's Attempt to Swim from Cuba to Florida," Todd, Pitlock, Reader's Digest, February 28, 2019.

[72] "The Man Who Ran to Atlanta," Euan Kerr, MPR News, April 16, 2010
https://www.mprnews.org/story/2010/04/16/my-run.

[73] "My Run Q&A with Terry Hitchcock,"
https://www.beliefnet.com/inspiration/interviews/my-run-terry-hitchcock-and-the-faith-to-endure.aspx.

[74] "O'Brien Delivers Keynote Speech at Big Ten Football Kickoff Luncheon," University of Minnesota Athletics, July 7, 2019,
https://gophersports.com/news/2019/7/19/o-brien-delivers-big-ten-football-kickoff-luncheon-speech.aspx.

[75] "4-time cancer survivor sees dream come true, taking field for Minnesota football," Enjoli Francis and Eric Noll, ABC News, October 21, 2019.
https://abcnews.go.com/Sports/time-cancer-survivor-sees-dream-true-taking-field/story?id=66429460.

[76] "Gophers placeholder Casey O'Brien shares positive news on his cancer fight," Andy Greder, Twincities.com, December 12, 2019
https://www.twincities.com/2019/12/12/gophers-placeholder-casey-obrien-shares-positive-news-on-his-cancer-fight/.

[77] "The Role of Deliberate Practice in the Acquisition of Expert Performance," Anders Ericsson, Psychological Review, 1993,
http://projects.ict.usc.edu/itw/gel/EricssonDeliberatePracticePR93.pdf.

[78] *Outliers: The Story of Success*, Malcolm Gladwell, Little, Brown and Company, 2008.

[79] "The Coach in the Operating Room," Atul Gawande, The New Yorker, October 26, 2011
https://www.newyorker.com/magazine/2011/10/03/personal-best.

[80] "Best Advice I Ever Got," Eric Schmidt, Adam Lashinsky, Fortune, 2009,
https://archive.fortune.com/galleries/2009/fortune/0906/gallery.best_advice_i_ever_got2.fortune/14.html.

[81] "American CEOs Seek a New Purpose for the Corporation," Alan Murray, *Fortune*, August 19, 2019,
https://fortune.com/longform/business-roundtable-ceos-corporations-purpose/.

[82] 87% of say stakeholders are more important than shareholders to long-term company success. "2020 Edelman Trust Barometer," January 27, 2020, https://www.edelman.com/trustbarometer.

[83] "A Fundamental Reshaping of Finance," Larry Fink, *BlackRock*, 2019, https://www.blackrock.com/corporate/investor-relations/larry-fink-ceo-letter.

[84] "Business Roundtable Redefines the Purpose of the Corporation to Promote 'An Economy That Serves All Americans," August 2019, https://www.businessroundtable.org/business-roundtable-redefines-the-purpose-of-a-corporation-to-promote-an-economy-that-serves-all-americans.

[85] "Leading the social enterprise: Reinvent with a human focus," 2019 Human Capital Trends Study, *Deloitte Insights*, 2019, https://www2.deloitte.com/content/dam/Deloitte/cz/Documents/human-capital/cz-hc-trends-reinvent-with-human-focus.pdf.

[86] "State of the American Workplace," Gallup, https://www.gallup.com/workplace/238085/state-american-workplace-report-2017.aspx.

[87] "2018 Edelman Trust Barometer," January 2018, https://www.edelman.com/sites/g/files/aatuss191/files/2018-10/2018_Edelman_Trust_Barometer_Brands_Social.pdf.

[88] "2019 CEO Initiative Study," *Fortune*, https://fortuneconferences.com/the-ceo-initiative-2019/.

[89] "From Purpose to Impact, Nick Scott and Scott Snook," *Harvard Business Review*, May 2014, https://hbr.org/2014/05/from-purpose-to-impact.

[90] Only 49% agreed…, "2019 Human Capital Trends Study," *Deloitte Insights*, 2019, https://www2.deloitte.com/content/dam/Deloitte/cz/Documents/human-capital/cz-hc-trends-reinvent-with-human-focus.pdf.

[91] "Workplace Trust – 58% Trust Strangers More Than Their Own Boss," https://www.onemodel.co/blog/workplace-trust.

[92] "Your best employees are leaving," *Randstad USA*, August 28, 2018 https://rlc.randstadusa.com/press-room/press-releases/your-best-employees-are-leaving-but-is-it-personal-or-practical.

[93] "65% of workers say they'd take a new boss over a pay raise," Ty Kiisel, *Forbes*, https://www.forbes.com/sites/tykiisel/2012/10/16/65-of-americans-choose-a-better-boss-over-a-raise-heres-why/#3afbe44176d2.

[94] "70% of employees say they are disengaged at work. Here's how to motivate them," World Economic Forum, November 4, 2016, https://www.weforum.org/agenda/2016/11/70-of-employees-say-they-are-disengaged-at-work-heres-how-to-motivate-them/.

[95] 75% say their bad boss is the worst part of their workplace, "8 Unsettling Facts About Bad Bosses," *HuffPost*, December 6, 2017, https://www.huffpost.com/entry/8-unsettling-facts-about-_b_6219958.

[96] "79 Percent of Employees Quit Because They Are Not Appreciated," Todd Nordstrom, Inc., September 19, 2017, https://www.inc.com/todd-nordstrom/79-percent-of-employees-quit-because-theyre-not-ap.html.

[97] "42 Worrying Workplace Stress Statistics," *The American Institute of Stress*, September 25, 2019, https://www.stress.org/42-worrying-workplace-stress-statistics.

[98] "Leading the social enterprise: Reinvent with a human focus," "2019 Human Capital Trends Study," *Deloitte Insights*, 2019, https://www2.deloitte.com/content/dam/Deloitte/cz/Documents/human-capital/cz-hc-trends-reinvent-with-human-focus.pdf.

[99] "Athletics at the 2012 Summer Olympics – Men's 100 meters," Wikipedia, https://en.wikipedia.org/wiki/Athletics_at_the_2012_Summer_Olympics_–_Men%27s_100_metres.

[100] "Leaders with purpose who communicate this purpose to their followers..." The Human Era @Work: Findings from the Energy Project and *Harvard Business Review*, 2014, https://uli.org/wp-content/uploads/ULI-Documents/The-Human-Era-at-Work.pdf.

[101] *How the Recession Shaped Millennial and Hiring Manager Attitudes About Millennials' Future Careers*, Career Advisory Board, DeVry University, 2011, https://www.careeradvisoryboard.org/content/dam/dvu/www_careeradvisoryboard_org/Future-of-Millennial-Careers-Report.pdf.

[102] *The Dream Machine*, Matthew Kelly, Hachette Book Group.

[103] *The Excellence Dividend: Meeting the Tech Tide with Work that Works and Jobs that Last*, Tom Peters, Random House.

[104] "Torpedo Annual Reviews Try W-5 Instead," Chuck Bolton, *Upsize Magazine*, http://www.upsizemag.com/business-builders/torpedo-yearly-reviews.

[105] "5 Employee Stats You Need to See," Maren Hogan, February 2016,

https://business.linkedin.com/talent-solutions/blog/trends-and-research/2016/5-Employee-Feedback-Stats-That-You-Need-to-See.

[106] *The Future of Work is Human: Findings from the Workhuman Analytics & Research Institute Survey*, 2019, https://www.workhuman.com/press-releases/White_Paper_The_Future_of_Work_is_Human.pdf.

[107] *Anxiety and Depression in Adolescence*, 2017, https://childmind.org/report/2017-childrens-mental-health-report/anxiety-depression-adolescence/.

[108] *The Path to Purpose: How Young People Find Their Calling in Life*, William Damon, Free Press, 2008.

[109] Physicians and Rural America, Roger Rosenblatt and Gary Hart, NIH https://www.ncbi.nlm.nih.gov/pmc/articles/PMC1071163/.

[110] *The Reinvented Leader: Five Critical Steps to Becoming Your Best*, The Reinvention Imperative Publishing, 2015, Chuck Bolton, https://www.amazon.com/Reinvented-Leader-Critical-Steps-Becoming/dp/150841078X/ref=sr_1_1?keywords=The+reinvented+leader&qid=1583341672&sr=8-1.

Printed in Great Britain
by Amazon

37655856R00147